SMALL CLAIMS COURT GUIDE
FOR ONTARIO

SMALL CLAIMS COURT GUIDE FOR ONTARIO
How to win your case!

Jennifer Young, B.A., LL.B.

International Self-Counsel Press Ltd.
Head and Editorial Office
Vancouver
Toronto   Seattle

First edition: March, 1973
Second edition: July, 1975
Third edition: July, 1977
Fourth edition: March, 1979
Fifth edition: September, 1983
Sixth edition: September, 1986

Canadian Cataloguing in Publication Data

Young, Jennifer.
    Small Claims Court guide for Ontario

    (Self-counsel series)
    First-5th editions by Peter Gilchrist; 1st edition published under title: Ontario guide to Small Claims Court.
ISBN 0-88908-356-8

    1. Small claims courts – Ontario – Popular works.
I. Gilchrist, Peter, 1940- . Small Claims Court guide for
Ontario.   II. Title.   III. Series.
KE01090.Z82G44 1986   347.713'04   C86-091134-9

you
1986

LSC 750
International Self-Counsel Press Ltd.
Head and Editorial Office
306 West 25th Street
North Vancouver, British Columbia V7N 2G1
Vancouver   Toronto   Seattle

CONTENTS

LIST OF SAMPLES

ACKNOWLEDGMENTS

The *Small Claims Court Guide for Ontario* has been improved as a result of suggestions sent in by our readers. It is hoped you will continue to help us with constructive criticism in order to make future editions even more helpful.

Thanks go to the following for their invaluable assistance: June Cardwell, Clerk, Toronto Small Claims Court; Peter Gilchrist, author of previous editions of this book; Russell W. Hawker, Administrator, the Ontario Legal Aid Plan; Steve McCann, Counsel, Policy Development Division, Ontario Ministry of the Attorney General; Ronald A. McFarland, Director, Provincial Court (Civil Division), and his assistant, Helen Walker; Georgea Wolfe, barrister and solicitor; and His Honour, Provincial Judge Marvin A. Zuker, Ontario Provincial Court (Civil Division).

And many thanks to two excellent typists, Jane Marshall and Peggi Warner, and a wonderful editor, Kathy Garnsworthy.

NOTICE TO READERS

INTRODUCTION —
HOW TO USE THIS GUIDE

There are many intricacies involved in any court system which, if not readily understood, often alienate the very people it was designed to help. It is hoped this book will solve some of these mysteries, while at the same time educating the layperson to be a better advocate, thereby saving both you and the court needless headaches and frustrations.

The small claims court is a court specifically designed to decide most types of "civil" legal disputes where the amount in dispute is relatively small. Civil law is the large body of law that resolves disputes between one person and another (whereas criminal law governs disputes between members of society and society as a whole). "Persons," in our legal system, generally include both individuals and organizations.

The small claims court was established in recognition of the fact that there are many lawsuits between individuals and organizations that involve a minor amount of money, but are nevertheless important to those involved. Most of these actions do not require the attention of lawyers. They need resolving in a speedy, simple, fair and inexpensive manner.

Many readers, no doubt, have had the unpleasant experience of trying to retain a lawyer for small claims court action only to be told that the cost of the lawyer's services would be more than the amount in dispute. One is left, then, in the position of either forgetting about the action or attempting to carry on alone. It is the aim of this book to assist those who want to go before the court without a lawyer.

The small claims court system is designed to be accessible to laypeople. It provides a means of legal resolution of claims and disputes without a great deal of formality, expense and delay. There may be cases where the skill and knowledge of a lawyer might be useful or even essential but, by and large, because of its informality, small claims court is particularly suited for parties to appear on their own behalf.

The staff at the small claims court offices are generally very co-operative in assisting laypeople to commence or defend actions. The fees charged by the court for doing the necessary paper work are quite low. (See Appendix 4.)

This book will in no sense attempt to tell you whether or not you should sue someone else or whether or not you should defend a suit against you, but, if you have decided to go to small claims court, it will guide you through the procedure and tell you how to conduct yourself at trial. In addition, once you have obtained judgment, it will provide you with a number of methods of enforcing that judgment.

Since this book is written for the layperson, an attempt has been made to restrict the use of legal terms. However, it has been necessary to use certain legal words because they often arise during the course of an action. These terms have been defined for you throughout the text and/or in the Glossary of Legal Terms that has been provided for you at the end of this book. To further assist you, some terms have been included in the Glossary that are not mentioned in the text, because you may come across them in the course of your action.

We have also provided you with samples of forms you may be required to fill out, letters you may wish to write and notices you may receive. You will be referred to these samples throughout the text and you may also locate them easily by turning to the List of Samples at the end of the Contents.

The samples are shown simply for illustrative purposes. Forms are available from the small claims court offices. The staff will assist you in filling them out.

If you encounter any difficulties, do not hesitate to ask the help and advice of the clerks at the small claims offices; you will find them particularly helpful. A list of these offices is provided in Appendix 3.

This book does not attempt to advise the reader on what the law is in any given set of circumstances and, in fact, could not, for such an attempt would fill literally hundreds of books. The same situation exists in regard to defending an action. There are many defences to various actions and it would require a large number of volumes to outline each of them.

It is important to remember that, although a lawyer's time is expensive, you can go to a lawyer with a specific problem and ask for 15 minutes or so worth of advice on it. In this case the fee probably will not be unreasonable.

You may make sure of this by asking ahead of time how much the lawyer will charge you. For example, you can retain a lawyer, present the facts of the case, and find out if it would be worth your while suing a person in small claims court. On the other hand, you could go to the lawyer and ask if an action that has been brought against you is worth defending. Once you have been given the lawyer's opinion and advice, you could then carry on the action yourself, using this publication as a guide.

There are other methods of obtaining inexpensive or free legal advice if you can't afford the $25 or so for a short interview with a lawyer in general practice.

The Ontario Legal Aid Plan sponsors a number of free legal advice clinics in the larger centres in Ontario. In addition, there are several privately sponsored free legal aid clinics. Finally, every law school in Ontario has a Student Legal Aid Society that will offer a competent law student to advise you (under the supervision of a lawyer) on your claim or defence.

To help you, a list of the legal aid offices in Ontario is in Appendix 1 and additional sources of inexpensive legal advice are listed in Appendix 2. Whenever a recommendation is made to see a lawyer, you should try these offices first.

If you are suing or defending in small claims court, you are not required to be represented. You may choose to have a lawyer or some other person, such as a law student or community legal worker, represent you.

If you have someone other than a licensed lawyer represent you in court, this person is called an "agent." If an agent appears in court on your behalf and the court determines that the agent is unsuitable to act as your advocate, the court may prevent the agent from acting on your behalf.

It is very unlikely that such an event would occur, but if it does, you should consider requesting an adjournment, so that you will have an opportunity to hire another agent.

If your small claims case is more complicated than average and you hire someone to represent you in court, you may use this book to familiarize yourself with the process that will be used to deal with your legal problem.

No matter which side of a case you're on, you should inform yourself not only of your rights, but also those of your opponent. The more you understand about the small claims court system, the better able you will be to participate confidently and effectively in the conduct of your case.

1
INTRODUCTION TO THE SMALL CLAIMS COURT

a. A BRIEF HISTORY OF THE COURT

The forerunner of today's small claims court was established in 1792 by the first parliament of Upper Canada.

The present system encompasses over 100 courts which hear three-quarters of all civil actions in the province. In recent years, over 100 000 claims per year have been filed in the Ontario Small Claims Court.

Only between one-quarter and one-third of these claims end up being resolved at a trial before one of the court's 350 or so judges. The rest of the cases are either not defended or settled out of court prior to the trial.

About three-quarters of all small claims involve disputes over unpaid accounts, loans and services. These and the other types of lawsuits dealt with by the small claims court are discussed on page 8.

b. RECENT REFORMS

In June, 1980, an experimental project was begun in the Toronto Small Claims Court. For the first time in Ontario, procedures such as pre-trial conferences and discoveries (discussed in chapter 5) were implemented.

In January, 1983, many of these new procedures became permanent features of the Toronto Small Claims Court system, and on January 1, 1985, the rules were extended to cover the entire province.

One important difference remains between Toronto and the rest of the province. As is discussed in more detail later, in Toronto you may sue for up to $3 000, whereas in the rest of the province you may only sue for up to $1 000.

The new rules have increased the size and types of legal disputes that may be resolved in the small claims court and have expanded the ways available to obtain information about your opponent's case, to conduct negotiations with your opponent, and to collect money or goods owing to you if you win your court case.

The new rules apply to all proceedings in the small claims court except appeals, regardless of when the proceedings were commenced. The result is that, aside from its relative informality and the size of the claims, the small claims court now operates very much like the higher courts in Ontario.

Another change worth noting is that, in recent years, much of the legal terminology associated with small claims court cases has been simplified. Up-to-date terminology is used throughout this book. For your information, the old terminology is included along with the new in the Glossary of Legal Terms.

An important legal reform occurred on April 17, 1985 when the equality provisions of the Charter of Rights and Freedoms became law. Section 15 begins "Every individual is equal before and under the law and has the right to the equal protection and equal benefit of the law. . . ." Any law that violates this right may be challenged.

An example of such a law might be the rule that if you live in certain parts of the province you are allowed to sue for up to $3 000, whereas if you live in other parts of the province you are only permitted to make claims of up to $1 000 in small claims court.

If you find yourself at a disadvantage in your lawsuit because the rules of the court appear to discriminate against you, you should consult a lawyer. (See Appendixes 1 and 2 for sources of legal help.)

A rules committee is empowered to make and change the rules of the small claims court, with the approval of cabinet. If you wish to make suggestions as to how the rules of the court could be improved to make the system more just, contact the following:

(a) Chairperson
    Rules Committee for the Provincial Court
    (Civil Division)
    400 University Avenue
    25th Floor
    Toronto, Ontario
    M5G 1S5

(b) The Attorney-General
    18 King Street E.
    18th Floor
    Toronto, Ontario
    M5C 1C5

(c) Your Member of Provincial Parliament

(d) The justice critics for the opposition parties in the Provincial Parliament

The judicial council looks after complaints made against judges. If you believe that you have been treated unfairly by a particular judge, you should seek legal advice before taking any action whatsoever. (See Appendixes 1 and 2.)

It is not appropriate to direct criticism toward a judge based on matters of personality. The only type of legitimate complaint you may lodge against a judge is in regard to his or her professional conduct. Criticism of the court system itself should be directed to the persons listed above.

You may write to the judicial council at Osgoode Hall, 130 Queen Street West, Toronto, Ontario M5H 2N5.

c. PARLEZ-VOUS FRANÇAIS?

The official languages of all Ontario courts are English and French. As of July 1, 1986, every party to a small claims court action has the right to require that the hearing be conducted before a bilingual judge.

The Ministry of the Attorney-General will provide English and French interpreters free of charge to parties. However, if you require an interpreter for a witness who speaks a language other than English or French, you will have to arrange for a qualified interpreter to attend court at your own expense.

d. GENERAL RULES OF THE COURT
1. Principles of fairness
The rules of the court, which are explained in detail throughout this book, are to be interpreted so as to result in the most fair, fast and inexpensive determination possible of every small claims court dispute. The court is to judge each case on its own merits and make a decision that is, in the legislature's words, "just and agreeable to good conscience."

If a matter arises that is not covered by the court's rules, the judge may make any order that is just. Furthermore, the judge may, where necessary in the interest of justice, decide that you do not have to comply with a particular rule. So, for example, if you were to be late in taking one of the steps in the action, the court might extend the time limit for you, depending upon whether this would be fair to all the people involved in the dispute.

The court is to focus on the real matters in dispute and not merely technical matters. Your lawsuit will not necessarily fall apart if some of the court's rules are not followed to the letter. While it is always best to adhere to the rules, if this has not occurred, the court may bend the rules for you in order to reach a fair resolution of the dispute.

In cases where the court creates or changes a rule, it may impose conditions on the person who is benefiting from this decision. For example, if you are given an extension of a time limit, you may be ordered to reimburse your opponent for any expense that is incurred by him or her as the result of the delay.

The court is not authorized, however, to make any decision that conflicts with any legislation. Therefore, it could not, for example, extend the time for commencing a lawsuit in the first place. (See the discussion of limitation periods later in this chapter.)

4

The Ontario court system encourages the resolution of legal disputes on a once-and-for-all basis. Therefore, you will not be allowed to split your case into two or more cases. For example, if you are suing someone because he or she borrowed some money from you and paid you back with a bad cheque, and he or she also has some property of yours and refuses to return it, this might all be processed as one action.

Similarly, if you're involved in a car accident with two other drivers, you cannot sue them separately, but must sue them together in one claim.

If someone sues you over a matter that has previously been resolved by a court, you may bring a motion to strike out the claim on the basis of *res judicata*. See chapter 5 for more information on bringing motions.

If you nevertheless do bring more than one action for damages, even if you are successful in all your actions, you would be denied costs except in relation to your first success, unless you could show that you had a good reason for suing more than once.

Also, you should understand the rule against "vexatious" proceedings. *You are not allowed to sue people for the purpose of harassing them. If you do so, you may be banned by the Supreme Court of Ontario from suing anyone in the province.*

2. Keeping yourself informed

The clerks and the other staff of the small claims court have a legal duty to assist users of the court. They are not permitted to give legal advice, such as whether or not you should sue, but explaining the rules of the court is an important part of their work. So, if you're in doubt, don't be afraid to ask.

Throughout the course of a case, various notices will be sent by the court to the parties informing them of hearing dates and decisions of the court. (These are described more fully later.) You are generally entitled to see any document that is on file in your case and, for that matter, any other civil court case. If during the course of your lawsuit you find that you are missing some documents that are on file at the court office, ask to see your file and make copies of those documents for your own files. You may be required to pay a small fee to cover photocopying costs.

3. Keeping your opponent informed

The official method for keeping parties informed of steps in the proceedings is called "service." In the course of a lawsuit, various documents are served (delivered) to the parties. (For further information on service, see chapter 2.)

As well, in most cases there will be some informal contact between the parties in the form of settlement negotiations. Events such as adjournments may require the parties to speak to one another by telephone and/or exchange letters.

e. THE BASICS OF A LAWSUIT

1. Whom may you sue?

Generally speaking, you may sue or be sued by anyone who is recognized as a "person" under our law. Legal persons include individuals and organizations, such as businesses. You may also sue the government, but as special procedures are required, you would need legal advice. (See Appendixes 1 and 2.)

However, some persons lack the capacity to sue or defend themselves. Minors (under 18 years old), individuals who are mentally incompetent or incapable of managing their affairs and "absentees" (Ontario residents whose whereabouts are completely unknown) are regarded as parties "under disability" who require special protective measures. An exception is made in the case of a minor who wishes to sue for less than $500.

If you get involved in a lawsuit and one of the parties is under disability, a "litigation guardian" (see Glossary) will have to be appointed to look after the legal interests of that person. You should seek legal advice to ensure that this is properly arranged. Otherwise, any agreement you reach with the person or judgment you obtain against the person may be overturned.

2. Basic terms

If you decide to sue someone and you commence a lawsuit in the small claims court, you become the "plaintiff." If someone commences a lawsuit against you in small claims court, you become the "defendant." The lawsuit is called an "action." An action is the entire sequence of events from the very first step in suing someone to the very last step.

Generally speaking, a plaintiff who is suing a defendant is asserting that the defendant did something or neglected to do something and, as a result of that, the defendant should pay to the plaintiff some amount of money either as damages or as a debt owed. The plaintiff is responsible for proving his or her assertions and must convince the judge of the truth based on the balance of probabilities. In addition to proving these facts, the plaintiff has the additional burden of satisfying the judge that, even if the facts are true, there is a legal obligation on the defendant to pay damages or a debt.

3. What is the deadline for commencing your lawsuit?

After a certain period of time, a person who has done something that might give you the right to sue is protected against being sued. This rule arose out of the idea that it is not fair to an individual to have the threat of a lawsuit forever hanging over his or her head. The legislature has placed limitation periods on all types of legal actions. This means that if you decide to sue, you must commence your action within certain time limits or you lose that right forever.

Some general rules regarding limitation periods are as follows:

(a) In an action for damages arising out of an automobile accident, the action must be commenced within two years from the date that the accident occurred.

(b) In an action for unpaid debts, the action must be commenced within six years from the date when the debt was incurred, *or* within six years from the time that the defendant last acknowledged the existence of the debt. For example, if you lent someone some money or sold someone some goods on credit in 1984, and that person makes a part payment in 1986 (or in some other manner acknowledges the debt), you have until 1992 to commence the action.

(c) In an action for assault, battery or false imprisonment, the limitation period is four years.

(d) In most other actions for damages, the limitation period is six years from the date when the damage occurred to you or your property. However, there are many statutes that put special limitations on actions where the defendant is a government body or a professional person. In these cases, the limitation period is usually much shorter. For example, the limitation period on actions against medical professionals is generally one year.

The best policy is to make up your mind as soon as possible after the event occurs and, if you decide to sue, to commence your action immediately. If you are unsure about the limitation period that applies in your case, seek advice from one of the offices or agencies listed in Appendixes 1 and 2.

4. What types of lawsuits belong in the court?

The power of a court to decide a type of legal dispute is called its "jurisdiction." The small claims court has jurisdiction over actions for the payment of money and for the recovery of personal property so long as they fall within the monetary boundaries of the court.

You may sue for the payment of money where you have suffered "damages" (a loss) as a result of a "tort." Torts are civil wrongs; the most common of these are breach of contract and negligence.

By far the most common type of dispute heard in small claims court concerns debts, each usually based on a contract. A contract is a legally binding agreement between two or more people that provides that each will perform some act, such as the payment of money, in return for something else, such as the performance of a service.

Actions on contracts include disputes over the payment of the contract price as well as disputes over the quality of work that was to be performed under the contract. Also heard by the court are disputes regarding unpaid loans and bills.

Negligence is also a common action. Negligence occurs when a person fails to take the degree of care that is required in a particular set of circumstances. It is often cited as the cause of car accidents.

Many landlord and tenant problems can also be brought to small claims court, but these are much more speedily and better handled through the procedures outlined in the Landlord and Tenant Act as explained in another Self-Counsel Press publication, *Landlord/Tenant Rights for Ontario.*

You may also bring an action to recover personal property owned by you which is in the possession of another person. But unless the property in question is one of a kind, you should consider making an alternative claim for the value of the property rather than for the property itself, as it is simpler to collect money than property.

Other torts are assault, battery, trespass, nuisance, false imprisonment and intentional infliction of mental suffering. If you are thinking of bringing an action based on one of these torts, consult a lawyer. (See Appendixes 1 and 2.)

Almost every action that the ordinary person may wish to commence can be brought within the small claims court system. If you are still in doubt as to whether your particular action comes within the jurisdiction of the small claims court, you should consult one of the legal services listed in Appendixes 1 and 2 or contact the clerks at the small claims court offices. (See Appendix 3.)

If you realize at some point that you or your opponent have launched the action in the wrong court, you should seek legal advice. You will probably need some legal assistance in arranging for the case to be transferred to the proper court.

5. Which court office handles your case?

In Ontario, there is only one small claims court which is divided into a number of territorial divisions. Each territorial division is a branch of the court and is responsible for carrying out the court's business in a particular geographic area of the province. There is a court office and a courthouse in each territorial division. The court offices are listed in Appendix 3.

Three factors determine which court office may handle your case:

(a) The territorial division in which the "cause of action" arose, that is, the territorial division in which the facts giving rise to the claim occurred

(b) The territorial division in which the defendant resides or carries on business

(c) The territorial division containing the small claims courthouse that is nearest to the defendant's residence or place of business

The choice of territorial division is generally that of the plaintiff. The plaintiff will generally want the case to be tried in the courthouse that is closest to where he or she lives or works. So long as this courthouse fits one of the above descriptions, this choice will be acceptable.

For example, if an automobile accident occurs at the intersection of Highway 27 and Highway 401 and the person who wishes to sue as a result of that accident lives in Oshawa while the other person lives in Oakville, the plaintiff has two choices: either sue the defendant in the small claims court that contains the intersection of the highways within its geographic boundaries or in the small claims court that has the defendant's address at Oakville within its geographic boundaries. If there is another small claims court that is even closer to the address of the defendant in Oakville than the court which has the address

10

in Oakville within its boundaries, the plaintiff may use that court.

It is frequently difficult to be certain which small claims court has jurisdiction in a particular case. If you are not certain which would be the appropriate court, you should phone or visit a clerk of the small claims court in your area.

If the defendant does not reside in Ontario, the action may be brought in the court that covers the location where the cause of action arose; that is, where the events occurred that led the plaintiff to believe the defendant should be sued. However, there are cases where the judge may decide that an action of this type ought to be tried elsewhere and consequently may refuse to allow the action to proceed.

Inquire at the court office as to whether arrangements may be made to serve your claim on a defendant who is out of the province.

The law surrounding the problem of suing people who do not reside in Ontario can become complex. Therefore, if you find yourself in a situation where extra help is needed, please see the references in Appendixes 1 and 2.

6. How much money can you sue for?

The small claims court is restricted to hearing actions where the amount claimed does not exceed —

(a) $3 000 (not including interest) in Metropolitan Toronto (including the cities of Toronto, York, North York, Etobicoke and Scarborough and the Borough of East York), & Ajax

(b) $1 000 (not including interest) outside Metropolitan Toronto.

These limits are known as the monetary jurisdiction of the court.

You may also claim interest. The amount of interest awarded will be based on the amount set out in any contract between the parties. If there is no contract, or if there is a contract but it does not stipulate how much interest is to be paid, then the interest awarded will be based on the

11

current prime rate of the Bank of Canada. The court will determine this rate for you.

If you win your case, you will be entitled to both pre-judgment interest and post-judgment interest. (See the Glossary for definitions.) The court will calculate these amounts for you.

The monetary jurisdiction was raised to $3 000 in Toronto in order to keep step with inflation and increase the accessibility of the court to people with relatively small claims. *The $3 000 limit may be raised in the future if it appears that there is a demand for this to be done. If your case is being carried on outside Toronto, check with the court office to see whether any change has been made in your area.*

You will not be allowed to split your case into two or more claims in order to sue for more than the official monetary limit. One set of facts gives rise to one action only.

If the amount involved in your claim is over the amount allowed, you have two choices. First, you may reduce your claim to the amount allowed, in which case the excess amount is treated as being abandoned and you cannot recover it. Second, you can sue in the district court, which has jurisdiction up to $25 000. In this case, you need to consult a lawyer.

Note that if the damages for which you are suing continue to occur after you have filed your claim, the judge will take the increase into account when he or she arrives at the final award, if you win your case.

7. How much will it cost you?

Since this book assumes that you will be going to court without a lawyer, the major expense in commencing an action will be the fee payable to the clerk of the court when issuing the claim. The procedure involved in issuing the claim is discussed in chapter 2.

The fee payable depends upon the amount you are claiming in your action. These fees vary from $6.60 (where the claim is under $100.00) up to $23.15 (where the claim is over $1 000.00). There is an additional cost of $6.60 for serving each defendant with the claim, and $1.10 is charged for each kilometre travelled by the bailiff in effecting service. (See Appendix 4 for the full schedule of fees.)

An action in small claims courts can usually be started for under $35. There are additional moderate charges in cases where you wish the court to subpoena witnesses. You can find out exactly how much you will have to pay by contacting the clerk of the court in which you propose to carry on your action. If you are a defendant in a small claims court action, there are no fees that you are required to pay before the trial, unless you wish to subpoena witnesses.

If you are the plaintiff and you are successful in your claim at the trial, you can recover your court costs, which include the cost of issuing the claim, service and subpoena fees and costs of collecting the judgment, if any. If you have had a lawyer represent you at the trial, the judge will often make an order that a fee for the lawyer be added to the amount that the defendant must pay you. This amount is not very large and would almost never cover the amount that the lawyer would charge you.

If you are a plaintiff and you are not successful in your claim at trial, the defendant can have the clerk of the court prepare an order against you ordering you to pay to the defendant any fees that he or she might have paid to the clerk of the court. Usually, there will not be any such fees. *However, if the defendant has had the assistance of a lawyer at the trial, the judge may order that you pay to the defendant a fee to cover part of the lawyer's charges.* The maximum counsel fee that may be awarded is $330. (See chapter 8 for more detail about counsel fees.)

The plaintiff, if only partly successful in his or her claim at trial, will still usually be entitled to the fees paid to the court clerk. However, if the defendant has "counter-claimed" (sued) against the plaintiff and succeeds in this claim or on part of it, the judge will often order that neither the plaintiff nor the defendant pay each other's costs and instead, each party will pay his or her own costs.

To briefly recap, if you are a plaintiff and lose the case, you will lose approximately $30 in court fees, plus any witness and/or counsel fees. On the other hand, if you win, you will recover these costs, plus the amount in dispute. See Appendix 4 for a full list of the applicable fees.

Regardless of the outcome, you will also be investing time and effort that you will not be directly compensated for. On the other hand, you will have the satisfaction of knowing that you are taking whatever action is possible to resolve your legal problem.

8. To sue or not to sue

To sum up the considerations outlined above, before commencing an action you should determine the following:

(a) How much do I want to recover, and if it is over $1 000 ($300 in Toronto), do I want to abandon the excess or bring my action in a higher court?

(b) Does the small claims court have jurisdiction to hear the matter?

(c) Which branch of the court has jurisdiction over the matter?

(d) Has the limitation period expired for bringing an action?

Last you must carefully weigh the amount of money involved and the chances of success against the money and effort involved in pursuing the claim and the risk of losing. It is not always an easy decision and the risk is always on the plaintiff.

2

HOW TO START YOUR ACTION — SETTING THE WHEELS OF JUSTICE IN MOTION

a. DECIDING WHOM TO SUE

You may sue as many people as you consider responsible for your legal problem. Thus, there may be more than one defendant in an action. Similarly, if the legal problem is shared by more than one person, they should sue together as plaintiffs. (For simplicity, plaintiffs and defendants are usually referred to in the singular in this book.)

If it becomes apparent after the action has been commenced that another plaintiff or defendant should be added to the action, you may bring a motion for "joinder" (see chapter 5).

b. IDENTIFYING THE DEFENDANT

It is very important that the defendant be properly identified. Before going to the office of the clerk of the court, you should be certain that you have the correct name of the defendant. This is particularly important when the defendant is a corporation. The following are several guidelines you can use in identifying defendants.

1. Individuals

A defendant who is an individual should be sued by setting forth his or her full name, e.g., Joseph John Smith. If there is more than one defendant, both names should be set out in full, e.g., Joseph John Smith and Sandra Jones-Smith.

2. Sole proprietors

A sole proprietor is an individual who operates a business under his or her name or a business name. If you wish to sue the business, you must name it in full, e.g., Smith Auto Company. You may also wish to sue the owner personally, e.g., Susan Smith and Smith Auto Company.

If you wish to sue a sole proprietor in his or her individual capacity and you are unsure about his or her identity, you should attach to your claim a notice to alleged sole proprietor, naming the person you believe to be the sole proprietor. (Follow the format shown in Sample #1.)

Also, send a notice like the one shown in Sample #2. If the business refuses to disclose the name of the sole proprietor as instructed in your notice, serious consequences may ensue. If the sole proprietorship is the plaintiff, its claim may be dismissed. If it is the defendant, its defence may be struck out. In either situation, a stay of proceedings (a halt) may be ordered. See chapter 5 for how to bring a motion requesting one of the above remedies.

3. Partnerships

A partnership is two or more persons who carry on business with the intention of making a profit. If you wish to sue, for example, a law firm, you will name the business name as the defendant, e.g., "Able, Careless."

If you wish to sue individual members of the firm, you must fill out a notice to alleged partner, which is the same as Sample #1, but with the words "alleged partner" substituted for "alleged sole proprietor." In this case, you might name defendants as follows, e.g., Able, Careless and Carl Careless.

If you wish to sue someone, but don't know whether or not the person is a partner, you may serve a notice on the partnership requiring it to disclose the names and addresses of all its partners (see Sample #3).

The partnership must comply with the notice or face the same serious consequences mentioned in the section on sole proprietorship above. If the partnership is the plaintiff, its claim may be dismissed. If it is the defendant, its

SAMPLE #1
NOTICE TO ALLEGED SOLE PROPRIETOR

NOTICE TO ALLEGED SOLE PROPRIETOR

PROVINCIAL COURT (CIVIL DIVISION)

Etobicoke Small Claims Court

Action No. 000/8-

Plaintiff:
Perry Plaintiff
234 Avenue Street
Etobicoke, Ontario
Z1P 0G0
234-5678

Defendant:
Day & Day Lighting Supplies
789 Industrial Road
Etobicoke, Ontario
Z1P 0G0
245-6789

Third Party:
(Fill in if applicable)

YOU ARE ALLEGED TO HAVE BEEN THE SOLE PROPRIETOR during December of 198- of Day & Day Lighting Supplies, named as a party to this proceeding.

IF YOU WISH TO DENY THAT YOU WERE THE SOLE PROPRIETOR at any material time, you must defend this proceeding separately from the sole proprietorship, denying that you were the sole proprietor. If you fail to do so, you will be deemed to have been the sole proprietor during the period set out above.

AN ORDER AGAINST THE SOLE PROPRIETORSHIP MAY BE ENFORCED AGAINST YOU PERSONALLY if you are deemed to have been the sole proprietor, if you admit that you were the sole proprietor or if the court finds that you were the sole proprietor at the material time.

February 2, 198-

Perry Plaintiff

TO: Donald Day
789 Industrial Road
Etobicoke, Ontario
Z1P 0G0

_____
Perry Plaintiff

defence may be struck out. In either case, the proceedings may be stayed. If a partnership fails to comply with your notice, you may bring a motion requesting that one of the above remedies be ordered. (See chapter 5.)

4. Corporations

If the business is incorporated, it will have after its name one of the following: "Limited," "Ltd.," "Limitée," "Ltée," "Incorporated," "Incorporée," "Inc.," "Corporation," or "Corp."

A defendant that is incorporated should be sued under its corporate name only, e.g., Happiness Inc. There are a few exceptions to this rule, but you are not likely to be confronted with them.

If the defendant is a corporation, you should conduct a company search in order to be certain that you have the correct name of the company and also to determine the location of the registered office of the company. You require the first piece of information because the name of the corporation must be exactly correct on your claim and you need the address of the registered office in order to tell the clerk of the court where the company may be served with the claim.

You may do a company search yourself by going to the public search office of the Ministry of Consumer and Commercial Relations, Second Floor, 555 Yonge Street, Toronto, and paying a fee of $2.10 per name searched.

You must provide them with the name of the company and they will give you a folder that contains the names and addresses of the directors and officers of the company, the correct name of the company and the address of the head office of the corporation.

If you're unsure of the name of the corporation, you should check the alphabetical list of corporations at the search office. If you require assistance, ask the staff.

The search itself generally only takes a few minutes. However, the search office is often quite busy, so be prepared to stand in line for a little while.

SAMPLE #2
NOTICE REQUIRING SOLE PROPRIETORSHIP
TO DISCLOSE NAME AND ADDRESS
OF SOLE PROPRIETOR

NOTICE

REQUIRING SOLE PROPRIETORSHIP TO DISCLOSE

NAME AND ADDRESS OF SOLE PROPRIETOR

PROVINCIAL COURT (CIVIL DIVISION)

Etobicoke Small Claims Court

Action No. 000/8-

Plaintiff: Perry Plaintiff
                    234 Avenue Street
                    Etobicoke, Ontario
                    Z1P 0G0
                    234-5678

Defendant: Day & Day Lighting Supplies
                    789 Industrial Road
                    Etobicoke, Ontario
                    Z1P 0G0
                    245-6789

Third Party: (Fill in if applicable)

YOU ARE REQUIRED under Rule 5.04 of the Rules of the Provincial Court (Civil Division) to disclose forthwith in writing to the below-named party the name and address of the sole proprietor constituting the sole proprietorship.

IF YOU FAIL TO COMPLY WITH THIS NOTICE your defence may be struck out.

February 2, 198-

Perry Plaintiff
_____
Perry Plaintiff

TO: Day & Day
    789 Industrial Road
    Etobicoke, Ontario
    Z1P 0G0

SAMPLE #3
NOTICE REQUIRING PARTNERSHIP TO DISCLOSE NAMES AND ADDRESSES OF PARTNERS

NOTICE
REQUIRING PARTNERSHIP TO DISCLOSE
NAMES AND ADDRESSES OF PARTNERS

PROVINCIAL COURT (CIVIL DIVISION)
Etobicoke Small Claims Court

Action No. 000/8-

Plaintiff:
Perry Plaintiff
234 Avenue Street
Etobicoke, Ontario
Z1P 0G0
234-5678

Defendant:
Day & Day Lighting Supplies
789 Industrial Road
Etobicoke, Ontario
Z1P 0G0
245-6789

Third Party:
(Fill in if applicable)

YOU ARE REQUIRED under Rule 5.04 of the Rules of the Provincial Court (Civil Division) to disclose forthwith in writing to the below-named party the names and last known addresses of all partners constituting the partnership of Day & Day Lighting Supplies during the month of December, 198-.

IF YOU FAIL TO COMPLY WITH THIS NOTICE your defence may be struck out.

February 2, 198-

Perry Plaintiff

Perry Plaintiff

TO: Day & Day
789 Industrial Road
Etobicoke, Ontario
Z1P 0G0

SAMPLE #4
REQUEST FOR CORPORATE SEARCH

Letter Search Office
Ministry of Consumer and Commercial Relations
~~Second Floor~~ *Companies Branch* *(596-3743)*
~~555 Yonge~~ Street *393 University Avenue*
~~Toronto, Ontario~~ *Toronto, Ontario*
~~M7A 2H6~~ *M7A 2H6*

Attention: Letter Search

Dear Sir or Madam:

                Re: Happiness Inc.

Please send me your report of a full search on Happiness Inc. In
particular, I would like the names and addresses of the directors, and the registered office of the corporation.
                                                    6.00
Enclosed is my cheque (or money order) for ~~$2.10~~, payable to
the Treasurer of Ontario, your fee for this service.

                        Yours very truly,

                        Irene Rate

                        I. Rate

It is possible to order this search in advance by telephone
and avoid waiting when you arrive at the office. (Call
416-963-0552). This search may also be done by mail. Then
it is referred to as a "letter search." For a letter search,
simply mail a letter like the one in Sample #4 along with
your cheque or money order payable to the Treasurer of
Ontario in the amount of $2.10.

5. Unincorporated organizations

The court may refuse to let you sue an unincorporated organization in its own name. It is best to name directors, trustees, managers and others controlling the organization's operations. If you cannot determine the identity of these people you may attempt to name the organization in your claim.

6. Car owners

If you are suing the driver or owner of an automobile involved in an accident, you should take careful note of the licence number of the vehicle and then write a letter requesting the necessary information as shown in Sample #5.

You will probably have the correct identity of the driver of the car from the information you obtained at the scene of the accident. Usually the driver and the owner will be the same person. If the driver is not the owner, you will want the owner's identity also because both parties may be jointly liable and you will increase your chances of collecting on your judgment by naming both parties in the action. For example, if one party has no money, the other may have enough to meet your claim.

7. Parties under disability

If you wish to sue a party under disability, you will have to name the litigation guardian in your claim. See the discussion of this subject in chapter 1.

8. The government

If you wish to sue a government agency, special rules apply, and you should seek legal advice. (See Appendixes 1 and 2.)

c. FILING YOUR CLAIM

Once you have decided which territorial division of the court has jurisdiction to hear the matter and who the defendant(s) will be, you should then go to the appropriate court office and complete the claim form provided there.

SAMPLE #5
REQUEST FOR IDENTITY OF VEHICLE OWNER

Records Search Unit
Ministry of Transportation and Communications
East Building
2680 Keele Street
Downsview, Ontario
M3M 3E6
Tel: 244-1115

Dear Sir or Madam:

Re: Ontario Licence No. DEF 321

Please send me an extract of the ownership pertaining to the vehicle bearing the above-mentioned licence, as of March 17, 198- (the date of the accident).

Enclosed is my cheque (or money order) for $5, payable to the Treasurer of Ontario, your fee for this service.

Yours very truly,

Sue Driver

Sue Driver

The clerk will process the claim and arrange to have it served on (i.e., delivered to) the defendant.

You are responsible for preparing your claim, so be sure to take with you to the court office the necessary information about the nature and amount of your claim, as outlined below.

The claim should be brief and expressed in your own words. It should contain the following information:

(a) Your name and those of any defendants

(b) The nature of the claim (You should provide as much certainty and detail as possible. You must at least include the date, place and description of the events on which the claim is based.)

(c) The amount claimed (You should include a dollar amount for the debt or damages claimed and also request interest and costs. If the relief you are requesting is the recovery of personal property, state this.)

(d) If you are handling your own case, your address and telephone number (If you are represented, provide the name, address and telephone number of your lawyer or agent.)

(e) At least one address for the defendant in order that a copy of the claim may be delivered to the defendant

If your claim is partially or entirely based on a document, then you must take a copy of the document to the court office, so that it may be attached to the claim. For example, if you are suing the defendant for a debt and you have a promissory note or a cheque or some other document that proves the indebtedness, you must file a copy of that note or cheque with the clerk of the court.

If you are unable to produce the document for some reason, you must state your reason in the claim. You should be aware of the rules regarding use of documents as evidence in court discussed in chapter 7.

As you can see from Sample #6, the claim instructs the defendant that there has been a claim made by the plaintiff for a certain amount of money and that the defendant has 20 days in which to dispute the claim. It also describes the particulars (details) of the claim.

If you chose a forum for your action in which none of the defendants either resides or carries on business, then you must file an affidavit in addition to your claim. The affidavit must state the reason for your having chosen your territorial division. The only acceptable reasons are that you have chosen the territorial division in which the cause of action arose or that the territorial division has the small claims courthouse that is nearest to the defendant's residence or place of business.

SAMPLE #6
CLAIM FORM

Provincial Court (Civil Division)
Cour provinciale (Division civile)

Ontario

SMALL CLAIMS COURT
COUR DES PETITES CRÉANCES

CLAIM/CRÉANCE
Form/*Formule* 7A

A.D. 19 8–

Refer to No./ No de référence	000	
Amount of Claim Montant de la créance	$	
Entry Fee Droits d'inscription	$	
Kilometers Kilométrage	$	
	$	

If you wish to file a Claim complete this form
Si vous désirez faire une demande, remplissez cette formule

WHEN REFERRING TO THIS DOCUMENT PLEASE USE NUMBER IN UPPER RIGHT CORNER
VEUILLEZ UTILISER LE NUMÉRO EN HAUT À DROITE COMME RÉFÉRENCE DE CE DOCUMENT

PLAINTIFF/DEMANDEUR

Name/*Nom*
POLLY PLAINTIFF

DEFENDANT(S)/DÉFENDEUR(S)

Name/*Nom*
DESMOND DEFENDANT

Street No./No et rue	Address/Adresse	Apt. No./No d'app.
	10 EASY STREET	

Borough/City/Ville/Municipalité	Postal Code/Code postal	Phone No./No de tél.
TORONTO	Z1P 0G0	234-1110

DEFENDANT/DEFENDEUR

Name/*Nom*

Street No./No et rue	Address/Adresse	Apt. No./No d'app.

Borough/City/Ville/Municipalité	Postal Code/Code postal	Phone No./No de tél.

To the Defendant/Au défendeur:
The Plaintiff claims from you $ 2 500,00 , and costs for the reason(s) set out below.
Le(s) demandeur (s) vous demand(ent) la somme de $ plus les frais pour la(les) raison(s) indiquée(s) ci-après.
**IF YOU DO NOT FILE A DEFENCE WITH THE COURT WITHIN TWENTY DAYS AFTER YOU HAVE RECEIVED THIS CLAIM,
JUDGMENT MAY BE ENTERED AGAINST YOU.**
**SI VOUS NE FORMULEZ PAS DE DÉFENSE À LA COUR DANS LES VINGT JOURS SUIVANT LA RÉCEPTION DE CETTE DEMANDE
DE CRÉANCE, UN JUGEMENT PEUT ÊTRE PRONONCÉ PAR DÉFAUT.**

TYPE OF CLAIM/GENRE DE DEMANDE:

- [ ] Unpaid account *Compte impayé*
- [x] Contract *Contrat*
- [ ] Motor vehicle accident *Accident qui implique un véhicule automobile*
- [ ] Promissory note *Billet à ordre*
- [ ] Lease *Bail*
- [x] Services rendered *Services rendus*
- [ ] N.S.F. cheque *Chèque sans provision*
- [ ] Damage to property *Dommages aux biens*
- [ ] Other *Autres* _____ (describe/donner un aperçu)

Reasons for Claim and Details/ *Raisons de la créance et détails:*
(Explain what happened, where and when and the amounts of money involved)
(Indiquer les faits qui donnent lieu à la demande, de même que le moment et l'endroit où ils se sont produits ainsi que les sommes d'argent en cause):

Between July 1, 198– and July 31, 198–, I built a porch for the Defendant. He

agreed to pay me $1 500 for my labor and to cover the cost of any supplies

required for the job. I required wood, glass, paint, etc., which cost $1 000. My

receipts are attached. I have made efforts to collect this money, but, so far, the

Defendant has not paid me a cent.

(Where claim is based on a document attach a copy for each copy of the claim, if it is lost or unavailable, explain why it is not attached.)
*(Si la demande est fondée sur un écrit, annexer une copie de cet écrit pour chaque copie de la demande, ou si celui-ci a été perdu ou ne peut
être produit, donner les motifs pour lesquels il n'est pas annexé.)*

Dated at/*Fait à* Toronto this/*le* 10th day of/*jour de* August A.D. 19 8–

Plaintiff's Signature/Solicitor or
Agent's Name/ *Signature du demandeur/
Nom de l'avocat ou du représentant*
Address/*Adresse*
3 Chagrin Avenue

City/Borough/Ville/Municipalité Postal Code/Code Postal	Phone No./No de tél
Toronto, Z1P 0G0	789-1234

CV 080 (rev. 11/84.

d. SAMPLE CLAIMS

For your further information, you will find below some examples of claims arising from different types of actions. They will give you an idea of the type of information that you should have ready in order to draft your claim. This is the sort of information that is to be inserted in the section of the claim form describing the nature of the claim.

1. Claim on an NSF cheque

"The plaintiff's claim is based on a cheque in the amount of $200 drawn by the defendant on the Royal Bank of Canada, dated July 27, 198-, payable to the plaintiff and delivered by the defandant for carpentry services on July 27, 198-. The cheque was returned by the bank to the plaintiff marked 'Not sufficient funds.' "

2. Claim for damages arising out of an automobile accident

"The plaintiff's claim is for damage to the plaintiff's car which resulted from a car accident on or about July 24, 198-, at or near 500 Yonge Street, Toronto, in the province of Ontario, when a car owned and negligently driven by the defendant struck the plaintiff's vehicle."

3. Claim for improper repairs to a motor vehicle

"The plaintiff's claim is for money paid by the plaintiff to the defendant for repairs to the plaintiff's automobile, carried out on or about July 9, 198-, at the defendant's premises on Yonge Street, in the city of Toronto, in the province of Ontario. The plaintiff claims that the repairs were either not done at all or were done in such a poor and incompetent manner that the automobile had to be taken to another garage for repair work of substantially the same nature as that which the defendant contracted to do."

4. Claim on a promissory note (loan)

"The plaintiff's claim is for a debt due on a promissory note signed by the defendant on March 1, 198-, and made payable to the plaintiff on April 30, 198-, or thereafter on demand. The plaintiff has demanded repayment of the loan and the defendant has refused to pay."

5. Claim for debt for goods sold and delivered and not paid for
"The plaintiff's claim is for the cost of a stereo sold by the plaintiff and delivered to the defendant at the request of the defendant to his premises on Yonge Street, in the city of Toronto, in the province of Ontario, on June 30, 198-."

6. Claim for debt for work done where payment has not been received
"The plaintiff's claim is for the cost of typing services performed by the plaintiff during the month of July, 198- at the request of the defendant. The plaintiff typed 100 pages of the defendant's Ph.D. thesis. The agreed rate of pay was $1 per page."

7. Claim for the recovery of personal property
"The plaintiff claims that the defendant borrowed a couch, a table, two chairs and a chest of drawers from the plaintiff on or about July 1, 198-. At that time, the defendant agreed to return the furniture to the plaintiff on September 1, 198-. The defendant has failed to do so despite several requests of the plaintiff."

e. NOTIFYING THE DEFENDANT
The defendant is officially notified that he or she is being sued by having the claim served on him or her.

Service of the defendant is carried out by the bailiff of the court. You must provide the bailiff with addresses for all defendants.

Service may occur by a variety of methods. One method is called "personal service." This means hand delivery, the surest way of getting a document to another person. Personal service may be difficult or impossible. For example, the person who is being served may refuse to answer the door or in some other way avoid service.

If personal service proves impossible at a person's residence, service may be made by the alternative method of leaving a copy of the document in a sealed envelope (addressed to the person being served) with any person who appears to be an adult member of the household and on the same or next day mailing another copy of the document to the person being served at his or her residence.

Personal service or the alternative method is only required for the plaintiff's claim. All other documents may be served by one of several methods. Where a party is represented by a lawyer or agent, the document may be served by mailing a copy of it to the lawyer or agent. If a party is not represented, it may be served either by personal service or the alternative method described above or by mailing a copy to the person at their last known address.

Claims of unrepresented plaintiffs must be served by the bailiff. If a plaintiff is represented by a lawyer, the lawyer may serve the claim. All other documents may be served either by the bailiff or by the party.

The advantage of having the bailiff do the serving is that you will end up with an affidavit of service sworn by the bailiff proving that service was properly made. The affidavit is usually printed on the back of the claim form, and is your proof that the defendant has been properly served. This will come in handy if the party disputes that he or she received the document.

The disadvantage is that you will have to pay the bailiff a small fee. (See Appendix 4.) You may be willing to pay this cost to save yourself the inconvenience of serving the document yourself. You may choose to serve the document yourself and make your own affidavit of service. If you choose this route, try to have a witness to the service, just in case any major dispute arises, despite your affidavit, about whether service occurred.

If you believe you have been improperly served with a document, you may bring a motion to set aside service (see chapter 5).

If you anticipate that the defendant may attempt to avoid service, you should be prepared to provide the bailiff with as much information as possible regarding the defendant's habits, such as his or her appearance, place of work, home address, recreation habits, etc.

You should keep in mind that if the defendant has moved from the address that you have supplied to the court or if you have supplied the court with the wrong address, you may have to pay an extra fee for the bailiff to make a second attempt to serve the defendant. You will be required to pay to the bailiff about $7 for each attempted service of each defendant. (For other possible fees, see Appendix 4.)

If service of the claim cannot be made upon the defendant because the defendant cannot be located or because the bailiff believes the defendant is evading service, there are certain remedies available. You can ask the bailiff to apply to the court for an order for substitutional service. If the bailiff obtains such an order, notification of the defendant will be allowed to take place by some other method than personal delivery, such as delivery by mail or by advertisement or by leaving the claim with a person who is likely to communicate with the defendant.

As long as the defendant is served by one of the above methods, the plaintiff may go ahead with the lawsuit.

The claim must be served within six months from the date that it is issued. Practically speaking, claims are served shortly after they are issued. But if for some reason your claim is not, you may bring a motion to the court to extend the time for service. (See chapter 5.)

Once the claim has been served, the defendant has 20 days within which to defend the action. (See chapter 3.)

If the defendant is not in Ontario, the clerk may be able to arrange for service of the claim, but the cost will be higher than usual. You will have to discuss it with the clerk, and you may wish to consult one of the legal offices listed in Appendixes 1 and 2.

3

WHAT A DEFENDANT CAN DO

If you are the defendant in a small claims dispute, you will usually have some idea of the nature and extent of the claim before the action is commenced either through oral discussions with or threatening letters from the plaintiff. However, the first *official* notice that you are involved in a legal action will be when the claim is served on you by the bailiff.

At this point, if you do not take any action at all, you risk losing your case by default. If the plaintiff obtains a default judgment against you, you will immediately owe the plaintiff the sum claimed, interest on that amount up until the time you pay and also the costs of the plaintiff in issuing and serving the claim.

Defendants would be wise to seriously consider all of the options described below rather than ignoring the claim and hoping it will go away; it almost never does.

a. COMPROMISING WITH THE PLAINTIFF

Consider what it might cost you to defend the claim and lose. If you believe that there is at least some merit to the claim of the plaintiff, you should give serious consideration to contacting the plaintiff and negotiating a settlement. For example, you could consider offering the plaintiff part of the amount of the claim in return for dropping the action.

If the plaintiff agrees to a settlement, you should obtain a release of liability with regard to that action from the plaintiff. A sample release form is printed as Sample #7. In addition to obtaining a release, you should also require that the plaintiff send a letter to the clerk of the court instructing that the action be discontinued. (See Sample #8.)

SAMPLE #7
RELEASE

No. 000/8-

IN THE MISSISSAUGA SMALL CLAIMS COURT

BETWEEN:

Paul Plaintiff

Plaintiff

—AND—

Diane Defendant

Defendant

RELEASE

KNOW ALL MEN BY THESE PRESENTS THAT Paul Plaintiff in consideration of the payment to him by Diane Defendant of the sum of one-hundred and sixty-five dollars ($165), the receipt whereof is hereby acknowledged, does hereby release and forever discharge the said Diane Defendant from all actions, causes of action, debts, accounts, claims and demands whatsoever which against the said Diane Defendant he ever had, as a result of (*put in here the events that led to the dispute between the plaintiff and defendant; for example, "an automobile accident between an automobile driven by the said Diane Defendant and an automobile driven by the said Paul Plaintiff at the intersection of Highways 5 and 10 on the 17th day of June, 198-."*)

IN WITNESS WHEREOF the releasor has hereunto set his hand this 2*nd* day of *September,* 198-.

_____
Wally Witness

_____
Paul Plaintiff

SAMPLE #8
LETTER INSTRUCTING THAT ACTION BE DISCONTINUED

September 10, 198-

Clerk
Mississauga Small Claims Court
470 Hensall Circle
Mississauga, Ontario
L5A 3V4

Dear Sir or Madam:

                    Re: Paul Plaintiff vs. Diane Defendant
                            Action #000/8-

Please be informed that the plaintiff has settled this action with the defendant and hereby instructs you to discontinue the action without judgment.

                                    Yours very truly,

                                    Paul Plaintiff

                                    _____
                                    Paul Plaintiff

It is important for you to remember that, while negotiations for settlement are continuing, the time limit within which you must file a defence is also continuing to run, and you should not let that time pass without filing a defence if you wish to contest the action. If you do not wish to settle, or if the settlement negotiations are unsuccessful, you should consider the remaining alternatives discussed below.

If you wish to settle, but your negotiations have been unsuccessful, file a defence to preserve your right to participate in any further proceedings.

b. FILING A DEFENCE

If you are served with a claim naming you as a defendant and you wish to dispute the claim, you must file a defence within 20 days.

You will have to go to the court office listed on the claim and fill out a statement containing the following information:

(a) Your reasons for disputing the plaintiff's claim (It is not enough simply to say, "I dispute the plaintiff's claim." You must be specific.)

(b) If you are unrepresented, your address and telephone number (If you have a lawyer or agent, state his or her name, address and telephone number.)

The court staff will assist you in ensuring that your defence is complete. You will not be required to pay any fee for filing your defence. A defence is shown in Sample #9.

One of the benefits of filing a defence is that the various notices that are sent out to parties by the court at certain stages of the proceedings are generally sent only to those parties who have filed claims or defences. The reason for this is that if persons have not formally stated their desire to participate in the lawsuit, it is assumed that they are not interested in the outcome. In order to be kept informed of all steps in the proceedings, parties must file claims or defences.

If you wish to file a defence but the 20-day period has expired, you may apply for an extention. However, you are unlikely to be granted an extension unless you have a very good reason for failing to file your defence on time. An example might be that you were bedridden during the filing period or for some reason never received the claim. (See chapter 5 for more detail.)

If you're a defendant and you wish to admit that you are liable for part or all of the plaintiff's claim, you may do so by filing a defence stating this. If you choose this course of action, you may wish to make a request in your defence to arrange terms of payment, so that you will not be liable to pay off your debt all at one time.

SAMPLE #9
DEFENCE FORM

Provincial Court (Civil Division)
Cour provinciale (Division civile)

Ontario

SMALL CLAIMS COURT
COUR DES PETITES CRÉANCES

DEFENCE/DÉFENSE

Form/*Formule* 9A

Claim No./Demande no

> **IF YOU WISH TO FILE A DEFENCE, COMPLETE THIS FORM**
> **SI VOUS DÉSIREZ PRÉSENTER UNE DÉFENSE, REMPLISSEZ CETTE FORMULE**

PLAINTIFF/DEMANDEUR

Name/*Nom*	
POLLY PLAINTIFF	
Address/*Adresse*	Postal Code/*Code postal*
3 CHAGRIN AVENUE	Z1P 0G0
City/Borough/*Ville/Municipalité*	Phone No./*No de tél.*
TORONTO	789-1234

DEFENDANT(S)/DÉFENDEUR(S)

Name/*Nom*	
DESMOND DEFENDANT	
Address/*Adresse*	Postal Code/*Code postal*
10 EASY STREET	Z1P 0G0
City/Borough/*Ville/Municipalité*	Phone No./*No de tél.*
TORONTO	234-1110

DEFENDANT(S)/DÉFENDE JR(S)

Name/*Nom*	
Address/*Adresse*	Postal Code/*Code postal*
City/Borough/*Ville/Municipalité*	Phone No./*No de tél.*

☒ I/We dispute the claim made by the plaintiff for $ 2,500.00 .... and
Je conteste/nous contestons la demande faite par le demandeur/la demanderesse d'une somme de $ *et*
costs. (details below)
des frais. (détails ci-après)

☐ I/We do not dispute the plaintiff's claim and wish to arrange terms of payment.
Je ne conteste pas/nous ne contestons pas la demande faite par le demandeur/la demanderesse et suis(sommes) disposé(s)
à m'(nous) entendre sur des modalités de paiement.

☐ I/We admit responsibility for $ .... and wish to arrange terms of
Je reconnais/nous reconnaissons mon(notre) engagement pour la somme de $ *et suis(sommes) disposé(s)*
payment, and I dispute the balance of the claim.
à m'(nous) entendre sur des modalités de paiement. Toutefois, je conteste le solde de la demande.

Reason for disputing the claim and details:
Motifs de la contestation de la demande et détails:

> The work that was done was unsatisfactory. The floor and windows are crooked.
>
> Also, the Plaintiff bought all the supplies in the most expensive store in the
>
> city, so her claim for the $1 000 is unreasonable. I counter-claim for $1 000,
>
> which is what it will cost me to have the porch put into good condition.

Desmond Defendant

Defendant's Signature Solicitor or Agent's Name/
Signature du défendeur, nom de l'avocat ou du représentant

Date   August 20, 198-

CV 324 (5/85)

If you make such a request, then a hearing will be arranged for you. You will fill out a financial information form and meet with a referee or other court official and the other parties. An order will be made, based on your ability to pay, as to how much and when you must pay to the plaintiff.

If you do not appear at this hearing, the clerk of the court may sign a default judgment against you. You should receive a notice of default judgment in the mail (see Sample #10). If a default judgment is obtained against you, then you will owe the plaintiff the full amount set out in the judgment.

If an order is made at the hearing to arrange terms of payment and you fail to make the payments as required under the order, the plaintiff may obtain a default judgment against you by filing an affidavit with the clerk stating the amount that was paid and the amount that was supposed to have been paid but was not.

Default judgment is discussed in more detail in chapter 4.

c. COUNTERCLAIMS

In addition to defending yourself against the plaintiff's claim, you may wish to make a claim against the plaintiff, which is called a counterclaim. This claim must arise out of the same events as the plaintiff's claim.

A typical example of when a counterclaim might be filed is if an automobile accident occurs and the defendant denies the plaintiff's claim for damages to the plaintiff's car and claims against the plaintiff for damages to his or her own car.

Another example would be where a worker claims for the balance of the contract price for work done for the defendant and the defendant denies payment of any more and in addition claims damages on the basis of shoddy work. This is the type of counterclaim stated on the defence form shown in Sample #9.

SAMPLE #10
NOTICE OF DEFAULT JUDGMENT

Provincial Court (Civil Division)
Cour provinciale (Division civile)

Notice of Default Judgment
Avis de jugement par défaut

Form/Formule 10A

TORONTO .... SMALL CLAIMS COURT
COUR DES PETITES CRÉANCES

Between/Entre   PENNY PLAINTIFF

000/8-
Claim no.
Demande no

Plaintiff/Demandeur

Nov. 15, 198-
Date of Judgment
Date du jugement

DANNY DEFENDANT

Defendant/Défendeur

NOTE: Take notice that default judgment has been entered in this action. (Please advise of further action to be taken).
AVIS: Soyez avisé qu'un jugement par défaut a été inscrit dans cette instance. (Veuillez faire savoir si d'autres démarches seront faites).

Plaintiff/Demandeur

Penny Plaintiff
2 River Street
Toronto, Ontario

Defendant/Défendeur

Danny Defendant
10 Ontario Street
Toronto, Ontario

Debt $ 500
Créance

Cost $ 20
Frais

Prejudgment Interest
L'intérêt avant jugement $ 10
(if claimed/s'il est exigé)

J. Clerke
Clerk/Greffier

30

When a counterclaim is initiated, two connected actions result: the main action and the "cross action." In the cross action, the defendant becomes, additionally, the "plaintiff by counterclaim," and the plaintiff in the main action is similarly known as the "defendant by counterclaim." There will usually be a combined trial for the two actions, since the cases are interrelated.

You may not file a counterclaim unless you file a defence.

You may make a counterclaim either by including it in your defence or by filing a separate statement with the defence. The clerk will assist you in filling it out. If you choose to attach it to the defence as a separate statement, you should follow the format of the claim form (shown in Sample #6 in chapter 2).

If the "pleadings" (claims and defences) exchanged prior to the counterclaim appear to cover all the facts that are in dispute, then there is no need to file a defence to the counterclaim. If this is not done, the defendant is not allowed to obtain a default judgment against the plaintiff. But if the plaintiff plans to raise new matters in court in order to make a defence against the counterclaim, then he or she should consider filing a defence to the counterclaim, so that the defendant will be forewarned about what will be argued in court. If the plaintiff takes the defendant completely by surprise in court, the defendant may ask for an adjournment in order to prepare a response to the new arguments.

In most cases, the plaintiff's original claim will make the facts clear enough so that a defence to the counterclaim will be unnecessary.

d. SET-OFFS

If a defendant is being sued for a debt and the plaintiff owes the defendant a debt as well, the defendant may request a set-off. This means that the debts would be subtracted from one another, with the balance being owed to the party who had the bigger debt owed to him or her and the other party being owed nothing.

For example, if the plaintiff proves that he or she is owed $100 by the defendant, and the defendant proves that he or she is owed $25 by the plaintiff, then judgment would be given for the plaintiff in the amount of $75. This simplifies the case, because otherwise two separate judgments would have to be given and each party would have to collect a payment from the other.

This procedure is only available where the amounts claimed by each party are easily ascertainable. For example, if each party had loaned the other a specific amount of money, these amounts could be set off against one another. But a claim for personal injury could not be set off, because the amount of damages would have to be determined by a judge.

If you want a set-off, include a request for this in your defence.

e. THIRD-PARTY CLAIMS

When a defendant wishes to make a claim against a person other than the plaintiff, it is called a third-party claim.

A defendant may make a third-party claim so long as the claim either arises out of the same events that gave rise to the plaintiff's claim or is at least related to the plaintiff's claim. If the claim and the third-party claim appear to be interrelated, then the court will allow the claims to be tried together, so that all of the related issues can be heard and resolved at one time.

An example of a situation in which a defendant might wish to make a third-party claim is if the plaintiff is suing the defendant for damages caused during a car accident. The defendant might admit that he or she crashed into the plaintiff, but would want to place the blame on a car mechanic who had fixed the brakes just prior to the accident. The defendant would want to join the mechanic to the action as a third party. Then, if the mechanic is found liable to the defendant, it won't matter so much to the defendant if he or she is found liable to the plaintiff, because the third party will be required to reimburse the defendant either fully or at least in part.

Of course, one need not admit the plaintiff's claim in order to make a third-party claim. In the example above, the defendant might deny that he or she was negligent but *also* claim that the third party was negligent in doing the brake job.

A defendant may file a third-party claim by going to the court office which is handling the case and filling out a claim form (see Sample #6). Then the defendant must give the clerk enough copies of the third-party claim, so that each third party will receive two copies and each original party to the action will receive one copy. The defendant must also pay a small fee.

The court will serve all the parties with copies of the third-party claim, so that all persons involved in the action are informed of this new development.

Any third party has the right to file a defence to the third-party claim with the clerk within 20 days of being served with it. Third parties must file enough copies of the defence so that every party to the action may be mailed a copy by the clerk.

Generally, the third-party claim will be tried at the same time as the original claim, but if the judge decides that to do so might unduly complicate or delay the trial or cause undue prejudice to any of the other parties, then the court may order that the third-party claim be tried separately.

Once a defendant has alleged that a third party is liable to him or her for part or all of the plaintiff's claim, then the third party has the right to join in with the defendant in disputing the plaintiff's claim. The third party will have a strong interest in having the defendant found not liable because then the third party is not liable to the defendant.

So, the third party may fight both the plaintiff's claim against the defendant and the defendant's claim against himself or herself.

Third-party claims are treated much the same as plaintiffs' claims. One small difference is that usually the third-party claim will be heard immediately following the plaintiff's claim. A second more important difference is that if a third party has not filed a defence within the required time and has been noted in default, judgment may not be obtained by the clerk. Instead, the defendant who sued the third party would either have to bring a motion for judgment or request judgment at the trial.

This rule prevents windfalls to defendants. A windfall would occur if the defendant won the third-party claim by default and then won at trial as well. Generally, third-party winnings are intended to indemnify the defendants against losses to plaintiffs. In other situations it would be more appropriate for the defendant to start a separate action against the third party.

The right to make a third-party claim exists regardless of whether the defendant promised earlier not to do so. Sometimes a contract signed earlier between the defendant and the third party contains a clause saying that if the defendant is sued, he or she promises not to sue the third party unless a trial has already occurred at which the defendant has been found liable. The law says that such a promise need not be kept. As soon as the defendant has been sued, he or she may add the third party to the action.

f. WHAT YOU SHOULD KNOW IF YOU'RE A CO-DEFENDANT

If you are a co-defendant, that is, one of two or more defendants in an action, and you are being sued on the basis that all the co-defendants are liable, you should be aware that even if any other defendants are found not liable, you may still be found liable.

This is called the "doctrine of joint liability." It most commonly arises in negligence actions and also under contracts that provide for this type of liability. When defendants are found to be jointly liable, each one is fully responsible for satisfying the judgment. For example, if Defendant A and Defendant B are each held 50% responsible, but Defendant A is unable to satisfy the judgment, Defendant B would be 100% responsible for satisfying the judgment.

You can determine whether you're a co-defendant by simply looking at the top of the plaintiff's claim. If any person besides yourself is listed as a defendant, then you are a co-defendant. If you are being sued on the basis of joint liability, this should be specified in the claim.

4

HOW A PLAINTIFF CAN
WIN WITHOUT A TRIAL

a. COMPROMISING WITH THE DEFENDANT

It is often worthwhile to try to get an agreement from the defendant that he or she will pay you an amount that is less than you are claiming in return for dropping your lawsuit. If you are able to settle out of court, you will save yourself a lot of time and avoid the risk of losing in court and being liable for damages and legal costs.

Chapter 5 describes the small claims court settlement rules. They are designed so that you have nothing to lose and a lot to gain by making an offer to the defendant.

b. APPLYING FOR QUICK JUDGMENT

1. What the plaintiff can do

If a defendant fails to file a defence within the 20-day period, the plaintiff may take action to get judgment without having to go to trial. This process is called "getting default judgment."

The plaintiff goes to the court office and shows the clerk the affidavit of service proving that the claim was properly served on the defendant. Then the clerk knows that the defendant is aware that someone is suing him or her and has been notified of his or her right to file a defence within 20 days.

Where the defendant was served in a different territorial division from the one that is handling the case, the plaintiff must prove that the defendant has been properly served with the claim, either by filing an affidavit with the clerk or by convincing a judge. If you have an affidavit of service, show it to the clerk, and if the clerk is not satisfied, he or she will arrange for you to have a judge make a decision on the matter.

If the clerk is satisfied that the defendant has been served, then the clerk will "note the defendant in default." This means that a note will be made in the file that the defendant has not filed a defence on time.

Once a defendant has been noted in default, the clerk may do certain things on behalf of the plaintiff, depending on the situation. If the plaintiff's claim is for a debt or for "liquidated damages" (see the Glossary) owed by the defendant, then the clerk may "enter default judgment" for any part of the claim that is undefended. This means that the plaintiff has succeeded in winning all or part of his or her case without it being tried. The clerk may award interest on the judgment as well, if the plaintiff claimed it.

It might happen that a defendant files a defence that answers some, but not all, of the plaintiff's claim. If this happens, the plaintiff may obtain default judgment on the part of the claim that is undefended. Then the plaintiff is free to pursue the other parts of the claim by going to trial. But once a defendant has been noted in default, a full-fledged trial is unnecessary. Instead, all that will be determined at the trial is the amount of the damages. The judge will presume that the defendant is liable to the plaintiff.

If the clerk enters a default judgment against the defendant, the clerk will immediately mail to both the plaintiff and the defendant copies of a notice of default judgment (see Sample #10 in the previous chapter), and the plaintiff may proceed to collect on the judgment immediately.

Default judgment is not available for "unliquidated damages" (see Glossary). If a defendant has been noted in default for such damages, the clerk will set a trial date and send a notice of trial to the plaintiff and any defendant who has filed a defence in the case.

If a defendant is noted in default for any claim other than one for a debt or liquidated damages, the claim must proceed to trial. When a plaintiff only obtains judgment on part of his or her claim, the clerk will set a trial date and mail a notice to the plaintiff and any defendant who has filed a defence.

2. What the defendant can do

Once a defendant has been noted in default, he or she may not file a defence or take any other step in the proceedings, other than bringing a motion to have the noting in default or the default judgment set aside, unless he or she obtains either the consent of the plaintiff or permission of the court.

Furthermore, the defendant who has been noted in default is no longer entitled to receive any further notices of any steps in the proceedings. *No notice of trial will be sent to the defendant.*

The one thing the defendant in this position can do is to bring a motion to set aside the noting in default or any default judgment that was obtained. The court will decide whether to grant the motion. If it does, it may impose terms and conditions, such as giving a deadline for the defendant to file a defence and requiring the defendant to pay some costs to cover the plaintiff's inconvenience and expenses resulting from the defendant's failure to file the defence on time.

One other thing the defendant can do is to try to obtain the consent of the plaintiff to have the noting of default or default judgment set aside. If the clerk receives the written consent of all the parties involved, he or she may set aside the noting or judgment. Unless the plaintiff feels that it is urgent to get the matter tried or believes that the defendant has not got a satisfactory excuse for having failed to file a defence on time and therefore is unlikely to be successful on a set-aside motion, the plaintiff might be willing to give this consent to the defendant.

The plaintiff has the option of refusing to give consent unless the defendant agrees to pay the plaintiff some costs and also, if a trial date has been set, agrees to an adjournment, so that the plaintiff will have time to prepare a response to the defendant's defence in time for the trial.

5

PRE-TRIAL PROCEEDINGS

The proceedings discussed in this chapter may or may not occur in your case. Every case is different and it is difficult to predict whether you will want or be ordered to participate in these proceedings. Each of them is different, yet each is designed to assist the parties to obtain the most speedy and fair resolution of their dispute. It is worthwhile becoming familiar with them, as they may provide you with some options that you may use to your advantage. The proceedings are motions, pre-trial conferences, discoveries, out-of-court settlements and statements of agreed facts.

a. MOTIONS

A motion is a procedure by which the parties to an action appear before a judge to determine whether the judge will issue a particular order.

A motion is not a trial, and the judge will not decide the "matters in issue" (i.e., whether or not there is a legal claim and, if so, for how much). The motions judge will merely decide whether the party who brings the motion is entitled to what he or she is asking for.

Motions may be brought prior to judgment being given in a variety of circumstances. Some of the more well known motions are listed below, but in any situation where you require clarification by a judge, you might consider bringing a motion.

Motions may be brought in order to obtain permission for the following proceedings:

1. Shortening or lengthening time limits

A defendant who has failed to file a defence within 20 days of receiving the claim might apply for an extension.

Or, a party who is scheduled to move outside the province in a month might want to bring a motion to obtain a trial date before that time. Limitation periods, however, may not be changed by the small claims court.

2. Adding or dropping a party to or from a lawsuit

These motions are called motions for joinder or motions to strike out a party, as the case may be. For example, if a defendant realizes after the time limit for filing a third-party claim has expired that someone else may be responsible for the damage that the defendant is being sued for, the defendant might want to bring a motion to join the third party. Alternatively, he or she might apply for an extension of the time limit for filing a third-party claim.

3. Obtaining interim possession of personal property

If a plaintiff believes that his or her property, which is in the possession of the defendant, is in danger of being lost, damaged or sold before the trial date, he or she may wish to bring this type of motion.

This motion may be brought *ex parte* (see the Glossary) where you have reason to believe that if the defendant knows about your motion, he or she will hide your property or otherwise endanger your chances of recovering it.

If your motion is granted and the property is handed over to you by the defendant, you will be obligated to take good care of it until the judgment is rendered at trial. If the defendant wins at trial and you must return the property to him or her, you will be held responsible to the defendant for any loss or damage occurring to the property while it was in your possession.

4. Amending a claim or defence

A party may bring a motion at any stage of an action for permission to amend or change a claim or a defence. After the claim or defence has been filed, a party may become aware of certain facts or laws that make it desirable to add, drop or rephrase part of a claim or a defence.

The court is required to grant leave to amend unless prejudice would result to another party, which could not be compensated for by awarding costs or an adjournment to the other party. Such prejudice might result if the effect of the amendment is to circumvent a limitation period that would otherwise protect a defendant. (See chapter 1.)

A person who is later added as a party, say a third party or a second defendant, is entitled to be served with any amended claim, unless the person is added during the trial.

The court is permitted to strike out or amend part or all of a claim or defence in the following circumstances:

(a) The claim or defence does not disclose a reasonable cause of action or defence. In other words, there does not appear to be any legal basis for the claim or defence.

(b) The claim or defence is scandalous, frivolous or vexatious. A scandalous claim or defence is one which refers to embarrassing matters that are irrelevant to the case, such as allegations of illegal or immoral activity on the part of one of the opposing parties. Where a claim or defence does not appear to have any legal basis, it is often struck out as being frivolous and vexatious.

(c) The claim or defence may prejudice, embarrass or delay the fair trial of the action. Prejudice means unfairness to opposing parties. Prejudice is often found in cases in which a claim or defence is so vague that the opposing parties are likely to be caught by surprise when they hear the details for the first time at the trial. Any statements that are irrelevant to the case are "embarrassing." Claims and defences that contain frivolous, vexatious or embarrassing statements, if allowed to stand, will tend to delay the proceedings.

(d) The claim or defence is an abuse of the court's process. For example, if it becomes clear that a party is bringing an action or defending against one for the purpose of harassing the opposing party, the court will not allow the party to proceed.

Where there is some basis for amendment, the court has several choices as to how to handle it. It may order that the action be stayed until a later date to give the parties time to revise their research and strategy in response to the change in the claim or defence. Alternatively, it may simply dismiss an invalid claim. Or, if the defence is invalid, it may enter judgment for the plaintiff. Finally, it may grant an adjournment and may possibly impose costs as well against the party that required the amendment.

5. Other types of motions

You may also wish to bring a motion in order to obtain permission for the following:

(a) Obtaining default judgment, if you're the plaintiff, or having it set aside, if you're the defendant (Default judgment is discussed in chapter 4.)

(b) Using commission evidence at trial (See the Glossary.)

(c) Obtaining costs against another party (These might arise in the context of a motion, a pre-trial conference, a discovery, an adjournment or at the trial.)

(d) Obtaining an adjournment (See chapter 6.)

(e) Arranging a pre-trial conference or a discovery

The motions mentioned above are best brought prior to trial, but if this has not been possible they may be brought during the trial. As well, certain motions may be brought after judgment has been obtained. These are discussed in chapter 9.

b. HOW TO BRING A MOTION

1. Time limits

Time limits are very important, and no one rule is applicable in all situations.

The first time limit applies to motions in cases when the party must bring the motion within a certain number of days before or after an event has occurred. Check with the court to see if there is a time limit for bringing the type of motion you wish to bring. Even if none exists, it is always best to bring a motion as soon as you determine the need for it.

Second, copies of the notice of motion and your affidavit (discussed below) must be served on all parties who have filed claims or defences at least seven days before the hearing date. The court will help you to arrange an appropriate hearing date.

2. Getting started

Every motion or application is commenced by preparing and filing with the court a notice of motion stating the nature of the order that you wish to obtain (see Sample #11). This notice of motion will be accompanied by an affidavit. You will be required to pay a small fee to the court for processing the motion.

Once the notice of motion has been filed with the small claims court office, it will be served upon the opposing party, who will then have an opportunity to cross-examine on the affidavit. If the opposing party does not take this opportunity, the motion will be heard before a judge on the date set in the notice of motion.

The party opposing the motion may file an affidavit stating the facts upon which he or she would rely in opposing the motion. It is open, of course, to the party who initiated the motion to cross-examine the opposing party on his or her affidavit.

Frequently, these cross-examinations and the preparation of the transcripts are time-consuming and the "return

SAMPLE #11
NOTICE OF MOTION

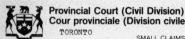

Provincial Court (Civil Division)
Cour provinciale (Division civile)

Ontario

TORONTO
.... SMALL CLAIMS COURT
COUR DES PETITES CRÉANCES DE

Notice of Motion
Avis de motion

Claim No./Demande no
000/8-

Plaintiff/Demandeur

Full name/Nom et prénom(s) Polly Plaintiff	Full name/Nom et prénom(s)
Address for service (street & number, municipality, postal code) Domicile élu (rue & numéro, municipalité, code postal) 3 Chagrin Avenue, Toronto, Z1P 0G0	Address for service (street & number, municipality, postal code) Domicile élu (rue & numéro, municipalité, code postal)
Lawyer or agent (name, address and phone no.) Avocat ou mandataire (nom, adresse, no de tél.)	Lawyer or agent (name, address and phone no.) Avocat ou mandataire (nom, adresse, no de tél.)

Defendant/Défendeur

Full name/Nom et prénom(s) Desmond Defendant	Full name/Nom et prénom(s)
Address for service (street & number, municipality, postal code) Domicile élu (rue & numéro, municipalité, code postal) 10 Easy Street. Toronto. Z1P 0G0	Address for service (street & number, municipality, postal code) Domicile élu (rue & numéro, municipalité, code postal)
Lawyer or agent (name, address and phone no.) Avocat ou mandataire (nom, adresse, no de tél.)	Lawyer or agent (name, address and phone no.) Avocat ou mandataire (nom, adresse, no de tél.)

TAKE NOTICE/*PRENEZ NOTE:*
A motion will be made to the court by *(name of party)*
Le/la *(nom de la partie)* présentera une motion au tribunal en vue d'obtenir

DESMOND DEFENDANT

for the following order *(Specify)*
l'ordonnance suivante. *(préciser)*

ADJOURNMENT

The following material will be relied on at the hearing of the motion. *(Specify, and where an affidavit is to be relied on, attach a copy.)*
Lors de l'audition, les documents à l'appui de la motion seront. *(préciser; et si un affidavit est utilisé, en annexer une copie.)*

MY AFFIDAVIT

The court will hear this motion at *(name and location of court)*
LE TRIBUNAL entendra cette motion à:au *(nom et adresse du tribunal)*

TORONTO COURTHOUSE, 100 JUSTICE WAY

on *(date)*/**NOVEMBER 10, 198-**
le *(date)*

at *(time)*
à *(heures)* **10 a.m.**

or as soon thereafter as the motion can be heard
ou dès que possible par la suite

Take Notice. If you fail to appear at the hearing of this motion, an order may be made in your absence.
Prenez note: Si vous ne vous présentez pas à l'audition de cette motion, une ordonnance peut être rendue en votre absence.

November 1, 198-
date

Desmond Defendant

party or solicitor/Partie, procureur ou mandataire

of motion" (the hearing of the motion) can be delayed some time until these cross-examinations are completed.

If you have been unable to follow this procedure, but wish to bring a motion at the trial, you should be sure to provide oral notice to the other parties as far in advance of the trial date as possible.

3. The affidavit

Except in the case of a motion brought during a trial, every notice of motion must be accompanied by an affidavit sworn by the party bringing the motion. The affidavit must state the facts upon which the party bringing the motion relies in asking the judge to grant the order. The affidavit must be made under oath. A form of the affidavit to be used is given in Sample #12.

For example, say a judgment was rendered against a defendant in his or her absence. If the defendant wanted to have that judgment set aside on the ground that he or she was not served with the claim, the affidavit would state that the defendant did not receive the claim and that it did not come to his or her attention in any way.

In another situation, if you wished to have discovery against a party, your affidavit would state that the information you wish to obtain, either answers to questions or a copy of documents, is essential to you in order to prepare for trial.

In another example, if a plaintiff wished to add another defendant to the action, the affidavit would state that he or she was unaware of the existence of that defendant or of the role that defendant played in the matters in dispute until after the claim had been issued. The affidavit would also state that, once the plaintiff has learned of that defendant or the significance of that defendant, the plaintiff had acted promptly to bring the motion.

It is important to remember that the affidavits must contain only facts and not argument. The argument will be made by the person bringing the motion before the judge, but he or she can only make the argument based upon the facts in the affidavit. Don't expect to win the motion by the affidavit alone. Simply swear to those facts that are necessary to enable you to win your motion when you present your arguments to the judge.

Another important thing to remember is that the opposing party has the right to cross-examine you about the facts in the affidavit. This means that that person can require you to appear before a court reporter and be cross-examined by that person or his or her counsel.

A transcript is prepared by the court reporter for use by the parties and the judge at the hearing. This transcript records all the questions and answers on a cross-examination. This is a common, although expensive, procedure, especially when the application is to set aside a default judgment. Typically, the lawyer for the successful plaintiff will challenge the assertion in the affidavit that the defendant was not served with the claim. If the cross-examination lasts for half a day, the cost will be approximately $100.

The preparation of an affidavit is a complicated matter. It is frequently necessary to obtain legal counsel to ensure that enough facts are being put in the affidavit to entitle the person to the order he or she is seeking to obtain. However, it is possible to do this without legal counsel, and the staff at the small claims court can frequently assist you.

4. The hearing

At the hearing on the motion, the judge will not be permitted to hear oral evidence from either of the parties. He or she is restricted to a consideration of the affidavits of each of the parties and the transcripts of the cross-examinations, if any, which have taken place.

Each party will be permitted to make oral argument either by themselves or by their lawyer as to why they should succeed in the motion or in the opposition to the motion. They may refer to the affidavits and the transcripts of the cross-examinations but no oral testimony will be heard.

SAMPLE #12
AFFIDAVIT IN SUPPORT OF MOTION

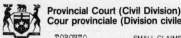

Provincial Court (Civil Division)
Cour provinciale (Division civile)

Affidavit in support of motion
Affidavit à l'appui d'une motion

Ontario

TORONTO.............. SMALL CLAIMS COURT
COUR DES PETITES CRÉANCES DE

Claim No./Demande Nº
000/8-

Plaintiff/Demandeur

Full name/Nom et prénom(s)	Full name/Nom et prénom(s)
Polly Plaintiff	
Address for service (street & number, municipality, postal code) Domicile élu (rue & numéro, municipalité, code postal)	Address for service (street & number, municipality, postal code) Domicile élu (rue & numéro, municipalité, code postal)
3 Chagrin Avenue, Toronto, Z1P 0G0	
Lawyer or agent (name, address and phone no.)/ Avocat ou mandataire (nom, adresse, no de tél.)	Lawyer or agent (name, address and phone no.)/ Avocat ou mandataire (nom, adresse, no de tél.)

Defendant/Défendeur

Full name/Nom et prénom(s)	Full name/Nom et prénom(s)
Desmond Defendant	
Address for service (street & number, municipality, postal code) Domicile élu (rue & numéro, municipalité, code postal)	Address for service (street & number, municipality, postal code) Domicile élu (rue & numéro, municipalité, code postal)
10 Easy Street, Toronto, Z1P 0G0	
Lawyer or agent (name, address and phone no.)/ Avocat ou mandataire (nom, adresse, no de tél.)	Lawyer or agent (name, address and phone no.)/ Avocat ou mandataire (nom, adresse, no de tél.)

I/Je soussigné(e) Desmond Defendant the/de/du City of/de Toronto
Full name/Nom et prénom(s) City, Town, etc./Ville, municipalité, etc. Name/Nom

in the/dans le/la Municipality de Metropolitan Toronto , make oath and say (or affirm):
County, Regional Municipality, etc. Name/Nom declare sous serment ou
Comté, municipalité régionale, etc. affirme solennellement que:

(Give facts in support of motion. Where the facts are not within your own personal knowledge, give the source of your information or the grounds for your belief.)

(Indiquer les faits à l'appui de votre motion. Si vous n'avez pas de connaissance directe des faits invoqués, indiquer vos sources de renseignements ou donner les motifs sur lesquels se fonde votre opinion.)

I HAVE NOT HAD TIME TO PREPARE FOR THE TRIAL DATE ON NOVEMBER 15, 198-.
I ASKED THE PLAINTIFF TO AGREE TO AN ADJOURNMENT, BUT SHE REFUSED TO
DO SO UNLESS I AGREED TO PAY HER $100 IN COSTS.

Sworn.......
Declare sous serment

Desmond Defendant

53

After hearing the arguments, the judge will either grant the order or not and, possibly, impose terms and conditions on the granting of the order. Occasionally, the judge reserves his or her decision until a later date.

5. Costs

Generally, no costs will be awarded to any party on a motion. However, if the judge hearing the motion becomes convinced that it was unnecessary for the motion to have been brought or opposed, or that it was the fault of a particular party that the motion had to be brought, then the judge may order costs against a party.

An example of where costs might be awarded is a case in which a defendant neglected to file a statement of defence. If the plaintiff brings a motion for judgment based on his or her claim against the defendant, the defendant might oppose the motion, arguing that he or she should be allowed to file a late defence. Even if the judge allows the defendant to file a defence, he or she may award costs of the motion to the plaintiff for the inconvenience caused because the defendant failed to file the defence on time.

If costs are awarded on a motion, they will not exceed $50 unless there are special circumstances. Such circumstances might include deliberate violations of the court's rules or the bringing of a motion in order to harass your opponent or delay the resolution of the action.

c. PRE-TRIAL CONFERENCES

Pre-trial conferences are meetings held by a court official and attended by all parties. All of the matters in issue are discussed in front of a referee and the parties attempt to reach a settlement. The referee is a court official whose job it is to try to ensure that the parties will openly discuss their dispute and make every possible effort to settle the case prior to trial.

In Toronto, all cases involving claims under $1 000 *must* have a pre-trial conference. Where a claim is for $1 000 or more, a judge reviews the case and decides whether or not a conference will be held. The practice varies outside Toronto depending on whether a referee is available. You will have to check with the court.

As well, as discussed below, even if a pre-trial conference has not been ordered by the court, a party may request one.

The pre-trial conference is designed to speed up the resolution of the dispute. Sometimes some of the issues are resolved or narrowed. If the parties find it impossible to settle the dispute, they will be in a better position, based on the information disclosed at the conference, to prepare for trial.

Information disclosed at the conference will not be disclosed to the judge or anyone else unless the parties consent. So, if the dispute is not settled before trial, the judge will hear all of the evidence and arguments for the first time at the trial. The referee is not empowered to make any final decisions regarding the case. Instead, he or she may make recommendations to the parties as to how they may resolve their dispute and it is the choice of the parties to accept or reject them.

The referee will give advice on how the issues may be simplified, whether any claims or defences appear to be unsupported and therefore unlikely to succeed at the trial, and whether some facts or documents appear to be so straightforward and accurate that the opposing party should consent to their admission at the trial.

When the conference is held by a judge, he or she may make orders regarding procedural matters, including —

(a) whether parties should be joined to the action,
(b) whether a claim or defence should be amended,
(c) whether a discovery should be held,
(d) whether some aspect of the case should be referred to a referee, and

(e) whether a party should pay some costs to another party.

When the conference is not held by a judge, the official who holds the conference may recommend any of the above orders, but only judges may actually make such orders.

Amending orders are quite commonly made as a result of a conference. This cuts down on delays that might otherwise occur and the costs that often go along with adjournments. (See chapter 6.)

A party who wishes to have a pre-trial conference must file a request for pre-trial conference with the clerk. Then the court will decide whether or not to comply with the party's request. If the court decides to comply with the request, then the clerk will arrange a time and place for the conference and send a notice of pre-trial conference to each party who has filed a claim or a defence in the action (see Sample #13).

Even in cases in which no party requests a conference, the court may decide that one should be scheduled. As in the case in which a party successfully requests one, each plaintiff and defendant should receive a notice. If any party who receives a notice fails to attend the conference, the court may make an order against that person for costs. Or, the court may make some other order, such as for an adjournment.

Further, if a person attends the conference, but is so inadequately prepared for it that the conference is a waste of time, the court may award costs against that person as a means of compensating the other parties for their wasted efforts. However, any costs awarded against a person at a pre-trial conference cannot exceed $50 unless there are special circumstances, such as harassment or use of the conference as a delay tactic.

At pre-trial conferences, all parties (or their representatives) are required to discuss all of the issues involved in the dispute openly and honestly.

SAMPLE #13
NOTICE OF PRE-TRIAL CONFERENCE

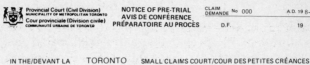

Provincial Court (Civil Division) MUNICIPALITY OF METROPOLITAN TORONTO **Cour provinciale (Division civile)** COMMUNAUTÉ URBAINE DE TORONTO	**NOTICE OF PRE-TRIAL** **AVIS DE CONFÉRENCE** **PRÉPARATOIRE AU PROCÈS**	CLAIM DEMANDE No 000 A.D. 19 8– D.F. 19

IN THE/DEVANT LA   TORONTO   SMALL CLAIMS COURT/COUR DES PETITES CRÉANCES

Between/
Devant   POLLY PLAINTIFF   **Plaintiff/Demandeur**

                              and/et

                    DESMOND DEFENDANT
                                                        Defendant/Défendeur

TAKE NOTICE: Pre-Trial of this action is to be held in the Courthouse
VOUS ÊTES AVISÉ que la conférence préparatoire au procès de cette cause se tiendra

at/*dans* 100 Justice Way, Toronto
commencing at 2 p.m., on the/*et débutera à le* 2nd day of/*jour de* October   , A.D. 198– .

Dated at/*Fait à*   Toronto   this/*ce* 15th day of/*jour de* September   , A.D. 198– .

TO/À   Polly Plaintiff   Desmond Defendant
        3 Chagrin Avenue   10 Easy Street
        Toronto, Ontario   Toronto, Ontario
        Z1P 0G0   Z1P 0G0

TAKE NOTICE – IF YOU FAIL TO APPEAR THE ACTION MAY BE DISPOSED OF WITHOUT FURTHER NOTICE TO YOU.

AVERTISSEMENT – SI VOUS NE COMPARAISSEZ PAS, L'ACTION POURRA SUIVRE SON COURS SANS QUE VOUS RECEVIEZ AUCUN AUTRE AVIS.

                        TRIAL COORDINATOR
                        ROOM 2214, 180 DUNDAS ST. W.
                        TORONTO, ONT. M5G 1Z8
                        965-6685

WHEN REFERRING TO THIS DOCUMENT PLEASE USE NUMBER IN UPPER RIGHT CORNER.
LORSQUE VOUS VOUS RÉFÉREZ AU PRÉSENT DOCUMENT VEUILLEZ INDIQUER LE NUMÉRO QUI APPARAÎT EN HAUT À DROITE.

If the parties reach some sort of agreement at the conference, the court official holding the conference may prepare a memorandum setting out the agreement and file it with the clerk. If some matters were agreed upon, but no final settlement was reached, the judge will be able to familiarize himself or herself with the parties' positions by reading the memorandum.

A judge who has presided at a pre-trial conference may not preside at the trial unless the parties consent to this in writing. This is because the judge will already have heard discussions about the matters in issue and may be disposed in the view of one or more of the parties toward a particular result in the case.

If the action is not settled within 15 days after the conference, it will generally be put on the trial list. When a date has been set, each party who filed a claim or defence will receive a notice of trial (see Sample #14).

d. DISCOVERIES

A discovery (also called an examination for discovery) enables the parties to "discover" the details of the case against them. Every party has the opportunity to question every other party on the facts of the case. While almost invariably used in civil actions in the higher courts, discoveries are a relatively new phenomenon in the small claims court.

Discoveries are particularly useful in complex cases, serving to clarify and possibly narrow the issues to be decided at the trial. Often cases will be settled prior to trial based on the ability of the parties after the discovery to assess their chances of winning at the trial.

The judge will determine ahead of time which matters may be "discovered." The judge will also determine what form the discovery will take. The examination may take place either by written questions and answers or orally. If it is done orally, the parties meet at an examiner's office and the proceedings are recorded by a reporter.

Because parties are questioned under oath at a discovery, their answers may later be used against them at the trial.

SAMPLE #14
NOTICE OF TRIAL

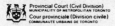 Provincial Court (Civil Division)
MUNICIPALITY OF METROPOLITAN TORONTO
Cour provinciale (Division civile)
COMMUNAUTÉ URBAINE DE TORONTO

NOTICE OF TRIAL
AVIS DE PROCÈS

CLAIM
DEMANDE No 000   A.D. 198–

D.F.   19

IN THE/DEVANT LA **TORONTO**   SMALL CLAIMS COURT/COUR DES PETITES CRÉANCES

Between/
Devant   POLLY PLAINTIFF   **Plaintiff/Demandeur**

and/et

DESMOND DEFENDANT   **Defendant/Défendeur**

TAKE NOTICE: Trial of this action is to be held in the   Courthouse
VOUS ÊTES AVISÉ que l'instruction de cette cause se tiendra
at/*dans*   City of Toronto
commencing at 10:00 a.m., on the/*et débutera à le* 15th day of/*jour de* November , A.D. 198– .

Dated at/*Fait à*   Toronto   this/*ce* 30th day of/*jour de* September , A.D. 19 8– .

TO/*À* . Polly Plaintiff   . Desmond Defendant
          3 Chagrin Avenue   10 Easy Street
          Toronto, Ontario   Toronto, Ontario
          Z1P 0G0   Z1P 0G0

TAKE NOTICE — IF YOU FAIL TO APPEAR
THE ACTION MAY BE DISPOSED OF WITHOUT
FURTHER NOTICE TO YOU.

AVERTISSEMENT — SI VOUS NE COMPARAISSEZ
PAS, L'ACTION POURRA SUIVRE SON COURS SANS
QUE VOUS RECEVIEZ AUCUN AUTRE AVIS.

TRIAL COORDINATOR
ROOM 2214, 180 DUNDAS ST. W.
TORONTO, ONT. M5G 1Z8
965-6685

WHEN REFERRING TO THIS DOCUMENT PLEASE USE NUMBER IN UPPER RIGHT CORNER.
LORSQUE VOUS VOUS RÉFÉREZ AU PRÉSENT DOCUMENT VEUILLEZ INDIQUER LE NUMÉRO QUI APPARAÎT EN HAUT À DROITE.

In order to obtain the right to have a discovery of your opponent(s), you must bring a motion requesting discovery. At the hearing of the motion, you must convince the judge that special circumstances exist that make a discovery necessary in order to achieve fairness. If the judge grants the motion, he or she will make an order as to who is to pay the costs of the discovery.

Discoveries are regarded as an exceptional procedure and will very rarely be ordered even if the facts and legal principles are quite complex. Generally, a pre-trial conference will be ordered instead. If the conference is unsuccessful, then a discovery may be ordered.

If an oral examination occurs, the party who made the motion requesting it will usually be ordered to pay the costs of the examination. These costs will include any counsel and examiner fees and the cost of the transcript.

If the examination lasts for half a day, the cost of the transcript will be about $100 *per copy*. The party who has been ordered to pay the costs of the discovery will usually be required to provide a copy of the transcript to every party who is examined and also to the court as soon as the transcript becomes available.

The party who has requested the discovery may also be ordered to pay the counsel fees of the parties being examined, if they are represented. Thus, the cost of a discovery can become quite high, and parties should hesitate and perhaps seek legal advice before bringing a motion for discovery.

If you are in a situation where it is particularly difficult to obtain information about your opponent that you need to pursue your claim or defence, and the amount of money at stake is quite large, then it may be worth your while to bring a motion for discovery.

e. OUT-OF-COURT SETTLEMENTS
Certain rules of the court encourage the parties to settle their case themselves, if possible. *Any party who receives an*

offer of settlement from another party should be aware of these rules or risk losing a substantial amount of money.

At any time after a case has begun, any party may serve on any other party an offer to settle. The offer would set out what the party is willing to accept in return for the case not going to trial. For example, a defendant might offer $350 to a plaintiff who is suing for $500 and additionally specify that the plaintiff must be willing to pay the legal costs of the defendant.

It would then be up to the plaintiff to décide whether to accept the offer by serving an "acceptance" on the defendant. In the meantime, the defendant has the right to withdraw the offer after it is made, in which case it would be too late for the plaintiff to accept it. An offer is withdrawn by serving a written notice of withdrawal on the party to whom it was made.

An offer that has not been withdrawn may be accepted any time up until the court has made a final decision on the claim. Once the judge has made an order for judgment, the order prevails over any prior settlement proceedings.

If an offer is made, but not accepted, the trial judge is not to be told anything about the offer until after he or she has made the final determination of liability. This is because if the judge is aware that the plaintiff, who is suing for $500, was at one point willing to settle for $350, he or she might be tempted not to take the plaintiff's claim so seriously.

However, the judge may take into account the settlement proceedings in assessing the parties' liability for costs. If, for example, a plaintiff receives an award that is only slightly higher than an amount that the defendant offered before the trial and the trial lasted for two days, the judge may decide to award the plaintiff less in costs than would normally be awarded.

If a plaintiff makes an offer to a defendant, the plaintiff may specify that the money to be paid by the defendant is to be paid into court. If the defendant accepts such an offer, he or she must notify the plaintiff once the payment into court has been made. Similarly, if a defendant makes an offer, the plaintiff may accept it on the condition that the money be paid into court.

These rules safeguard the plaintiff against broken promises by the defendant. After all, if the dispute between them has proceeded to this stage, then the defendant was probably unwilling to settle the matter earlier and the plaintiff may be suspicious about the defendant's change of mind. By having money paid into court, a party may verify whether the opposing party has lived up to his or her end of the bargain. As well, the court then has a record of the settlement and can proceed to take the case off the trial list.

If an offer to settle is accepted, but does not specify who is to be responsible for the legal costs, then certain rules apply. If the defendant made the offer, then the plaintiff is entitled to be paid his or her disbursements incurred up to the date when he or she was served with the offer made by the defendant. If the plaintiff made the offer, he or she is entitled to receive money covering his or her disbursements incurred up to the date that the notice of acceptance was served.

The reason behind these rules is that the fact that an offer was made and accepted shows that the money spent earlier on the case was unnecessary.

If a party who has accepted an offer to settle fails to keep the bargain, the other party has a choice: he or she may make a motion to the court for judgment according to the terms of the accepted offer, or he or she may opt to continue the proceedings and go to trial as if there had not been an offer to settle.

If a defendant has agreed to pay money into court and fails to do so, then the plaintiff has these same options.

When a party is served with an offer to settle, the party should seriously consider whether he or she is likely to obtain more money by proceeding to trial. If the chances of this are slim, the party should probably accept the offer. If the party does not accept an offer and the judge awards an amount that is less than the party would have received if he or she had accepted the offer, the party may be required to pay some costs of the opponent, *even if he or she wins the case.* case.

If either party makes an offer *at least seven days before the trial* and the offer is neither withdrawn nor accepted, and then the party to whom the offer was made obtains a judgment that is no better than the offer, the court may award the party who made the offer costs, *even if this party loses the case.*

In these circumstances, the court can award the party who had made the offer *up to twice the costs of the winner* of the action. For example, if the plaintiff had made an offer that was not accepted by the defendant and then recovered a greater amount at trial, he or she might be awarded double the usual costs. Similarly, if the plaintiff loses, or wins but recovers no more than the defendant had offered, the defendant may recover double costs.

If this type of award is made to a party who is unrepresented by counsel, then the court may additionally award the party who had made the offer up to $300 in compensation for the inconvenience and expense caused by having to go through the trial.

If an offer to settle is made less than seven days before the trial, then none of the penalty provisions regarding costs just discussed apply. Parties are entitled to a reasonable length of time to make up their minds about possible settlement. To get the full benefit of the rules regarding settlement, parties should know what they might be willing to settle for long before the week before the trial.

Keep in mind that in the vast majority of cases, people are able to reach a compromise prior to trial. However, if settlement proceedings are occurring, but no agreement has yet been reached, you should read about trial preparation.

If you are interested in settling your case, but the workings of the settlement rules are beyond your grasp, you should seek legal assistance.

You should also know that parties may at any time agree to any settlement on any terms that are acceptable to both parties. The court won't get involved unless a party is "under disability." (See chapter 1.)

If you reach a settlement prior to the trial date, advise the trial co-ordinator that you wish to have your case struck off the trial list.

f. STATEMENTS OF AGREED FACTS

Statements of agreed facts are statements containing a list of the facts of a case that the parties agree upon, eliminating the need for either party to present any evidence in relation to these facts at the trial.

Sometimes the court will request that the parties try to reach an agreement of facts. If you receive such a request, contact the other side and go over all the facts contained in your claim and defence. Give your agreement only to those facts asserted by your opponent that you have no chance of disproving.

If you are able to reach an agreement, you will submit the statement to the court prior to the trial date. Then the judge who hears the case will know what evidence is necessary and what is not. Agreed statements of fact simplify and shorten the trial.

6

HOW TO PREPARE
FOR THE TRIAL

Law professors, experienced lawyers and judges all agree that trial preparation is the key to successful advocacy. The better prepared you are, the more reason you will have to feel confident in court.

a. SETTING THE TRIAL DATE

Unless a pre-trial conference is to be held, the clerk will set a date for the trial and send a notice of trial to every party who has filed a claim or a defence.

If a pre-trial conference is to be held, the clerk will wait until the outcome of the pre-trial conference is known. If no settlement is reached at the conference, then a trial date will be set and notice sent out.

As shown in Sample #14 in chapter 5, this notice states the time, date, and place where the trial is to be held. Check the address given for the trial, as the court may be located in a building other than the court office.

If your case is to be heard in Toronto and the amount of the claim is $500 or less, you may schedule your trial in the evening rather than during regular business hours. (Contact the trial co-ordinator at 965-6685 to arrange for an evening trial.)

In busy parts of the province, such as Toronto, you may have to wait a couple of months to get a trial date. From the time you receive your notice of trial, you will probably have about a month to wait. If you wish to get an approximate idea in advance as to how far ahead your trial date will be and therefore how much time you have to prepare for your trial, contact the trial co-ordinator for the court office that is handling your case.

Once the parties have received the notice of trial, they should prepare themselves for court, as discussed below.

b. WHAT THE PLAINTIFF SHOULD DO

The plaintiff, of course, will have a pretty good idea of what must be established at trial, having carefully considered the position before the claim was issued. It is very helpful to make a written list of the facts you feel will be essential to your case and to note beside them how you propose to prove each fact.

Remember that, although the judge will be helpful and will not hold you to the strict formalities of the higher courts, he or she cannot be expected to reach a decision in your favor unless presented with all the facts necessary to establish your case.

For example, if your claim is based upon a contract, you must prove to the court that the contract was openly and freely made between you and the defendant and that certain conditions in it were not performed or only partly performed or not performed satisfactorily. If the contract was a written one, you should have your copy to present to the judge at the trial. If the contract was oral, you will have to testify that a contract exists. If the defendant is going to deny that there was a contract, it will help you to have a witness ready to testify on your behalf. But keep in mind the ground rules for what is acceptable evidence and what is not. (See chapter 8.)

Sometimes your proof that a contract existed is that there has been "part performance" by the other party. In these cases you may not require a witness. For example, suppose you orally contract with a plumber to install an extra bathroom in the recreation room at a certain price and the plumber proceeds to take out part of the wall and then decides the job is too much trouble for the agreed figure. At this point you are at liberty to obtain estimates from other plumbers and sue the first plumber for the difference. It would be hard for the first plumber to deny there was a contract because the work had already been partly completed.

The procedure for ensuring that the witnesses attend the trial is discussed in chapter 7. The method of proof you use to show that the contract was not completed will vary according to what it is that the defendant was supposed to do.

If the defendant was supposed to pay you money for something you did, you need simply assert in court that you have received no payment. Once you have shown that you did what you were supposed to do for the money, it will be up to the defendant to prove that some payment has been made. The defendant may deny that what you did was worth that money, and you should be prepared to provide proof, such as some written record of the hours you spent doing the work and the cost of the materials that you used in order to support the claim, and you should be able to call witnesses if possible.

It is a good idea to keep a diary of all events related to your case, such as conversations with your opponent. You may later be able to use it to refresh your memory when testifying in court. However, unless your notes are made at the time or shortly after the events occur, your opponent may challenge your recollection of the events.

If the defendant was supposed to do some work for you and did not do so, you can support your claim that the work was not done by your testimony, photographs, or other similar documents.

Be sure to have enough copies of any documents you plan to use in court to give one to each party and one to the judge. It's a good idea to have one extra copy for such purposes as showing it to a witness who is familiar with it and can answer questions about it.

Other types of actions will require different types of proof. You may simply analyze any situation by using the following process. In most cases, the plaintiff is asserting that the defendant had some type of duty to do something or not to do something and that the defendant violated that duty in some way. The plaintiff is also asserting that because the defendant violated that duty, the plaintiff has suffered some damage or is owed some money. If the problem is approached in this manner, you can usually determine what it is you have to show to the judge.

First, you should arrange the facts in some type of sensible order. Chronological order is usually the most satisfactory. Leave yourself some space beside each fact to make notes at trial.

Having completed your list of facts, you should decide in what order you are going to call your witnesses, if you have any. It is usually advisable to put your best witness on first. This way, you have a good chance of making a favorable first impression on the court. You are often your own best witness, since you may be the only person in a position to give a full account of the events leading up to the dispute.

You should then speak to your other witnesses and go over the questions you intend to ask them. There is nothing improper in this, as long as you do not coach them as to what to say in court, and there is no need for your witnesses to deny that they co-operated in this manner if cross-examined on the matter. You should warn your witnesses that they will be giving sworn testimony and that if they lie in the witness box, they may be prosecuted for perjury. Advise them to relax as much as possible and simply tell the truth to the best of their recollection. If they are unsure of any information, they should say so.

It will be very helpful to you to make up a list of questions you wish to ask each witness. Design them so as to encourage him or her to answer you by giving the information you wish the judge to hear. See chapter 8 to find out what sort of questions you are permitted to ask of a witness in court.

c. WHAT THE DEFENDANT SHOULD DO

For the defendant, the procedure is similar except that it is done in reverse. If you are the defendant and have decided to fight, you must have a legal defence to the action. In other words, it is simply not good enough to say, "I don't like his way of doing business," and not pay the bill. You must have, or at least think you have, a legal defence.

Generally, you may be denying that you ever had a duty to do or you may be denying that you failed to do your duty. Alternatively, or in addition, you may be denying that the plaintiff suffered any damages or is owed any money as a result of your action. You should consider your version of the facts and make a list. Beside each fact, note how you are planning to prove it.

You should prepare your witnesses just as the plaintiff has and remember to obtain any documents you will be referring to in your case and have enough copies on hand to be able to use them in court.

You might also consider keeping a diary from the time when you became aware that you may end up in court. See the discussion in the previous section.

d. HOW TO CHANGE THE TRIAL DATE

You may discover that it is impossible to appear in court on the date scheduled for trial or surprises arise between the setting of the trial date and the trial itself which make it difficult for you to prepare adequately for the trial. In such cases, you may wish to postpone the trial date. Such a postponement is called an adjournment.

On the other hand, an emergency might arise that would make it desirable for you to have the trial occur sooner. For example, you might learn that your opponent is planning to leave the country prior to the time when the trial would normally take place. If you're in this position, you might consider bringing a motion to have the case moved up on the trial list.

If you want an adjournment, you should seek the consent of the other party. If there is more than one defendant, or if a third party is involved, the consent of all of them is required.

If consent is obtained, you must mail a letter to the clerk of the small claims court informing the clerk that the other parties have consented to an adjournment and requesting a new trial date.

If the parties have been making headway in negotiations and feel that the case will likely be settled in the near future, they may wish to have the case adjourned indefinitely. If this situation occurs, no new trial date will be sought, but the parties can agree that the action may be resumed at the request of any party, so long as a reasonable period of notice, say two weeks, is given to the other parties. This way, if negotiations break down, the action may be picked up where it was left off. The court office would be notified and a new trial date would be set.

If the other party will not consent to an adjournment, you should notify the other party by registered mail that an adjournment will be sought. Be sure to keep the registration slip and a copy of your letter. Then, when the trial date arrives, you can make this request to the judge and can show the judge that the other parties were notified that this request would be made.

Adjournments are almost invariably granted the first time around, especially if the other parties have been notified in advance. However, you may be ordered to pay any witness costs of the other parties.

Second and subsequent adjournments, if contested, are more difficult to obtain and you should have very good reasons to present to the judge. Examples of these might be if you unexpectedly become seriously ill or if an important witness is unavailable on the scheduled trial date.

Adjournments tend to throw the court's schedule "out of whack" and also inconvenience witnesses who arrive at court expecting the trial to take place. If the consent of all parties is obtained, however, there should be no problem arranging an adjournment, so long as the court is notified early enough to reschedule other cases.

If the court is not notified far enough in advance, the parties may be required to appear in court on the scheduled trial date and formally request an adjournment from the judge. So, it is a good idea to ask yourself a few weeks before the trial date whether or not you will be requiring an adjournment.

If your case is to be heard in Toronto, you must notify the trial co-ordinator that you want an adjournment at least two weeks before the scheduled trial date. You will have to send a letter to the trial co-ordinator showing that you have obtained the consent of all parties.

As a matter of courtesy, if an adjournment is obtained, all witnesses should be notified, so that they do not attend at court unnecessarily. If you do not do so, you may be ordered to compensate them for their inconvenience and expense. This could include loss of income and travel costs. Also, you will have to inform the witnesses of the new trial date.

Similarly, if an adjournment is obtained in court without all of the parties being present, you will have to notify all absent parties of the new trial date. The court will not automatically do this.

If the plaintiff waits for the trial date to ask for an adjournment, the judge may choose to adjourn the case indefinitely. If the defendant requests an adjournment on the trial date, the judge may order that the new trial date will be "peremptory" to all parties. This means that no further adjournment will be granted and all parties must show up on the new trial date or lose their right to participate in the case.

e. HOW TO CANCEL THE TRIAL

If the plaintiff decides before the date set for trial not to proceed with the trial, he or she should contact the defendant and ask the defendant to consent to a discontinuance of the action without costs. If the defendant agrees, the plaintiff should advise the court clerk in writing that the defendant has consented to a discontinuance and that the plaintiff wishes to discontinue. (An example of such a letter was shown as Sample #8 in chapter 3.)

If the defendant refuses to abandon the action without costs, the plaintiff should send the defendant a registered letter saying that he or she is going to request the judge to dismiss the action at trial; the plaintiff should keep the registration slip and a copy of the letter.

After receiving such an official notice the defendant will not be able to claim costs for witnesses if he or she ignores the notice and brings them anyway. The plaintiff will, however, normally be responsible for the other court costs of the defendant's witnesses if they have not been notified of the plaintiff's intention to request a dismissal. In any event, these costs are minimal. (See Appendix 4.)

If you are the defendant and decide to discontinue your defence, you need merely notify the clerk of the small claims court and judgment will be entered against you.

7

WITNESSES

a. DO YOU NEED ANY WITNESSES?

If no defence is filed to a claim, the plaintiff may prove his or her case simply by filing an affidavit if the judge allows this. If permission is given, then the plaintiff need not call any witnesses nor testify himself or herself in order to win the case.

Certain statements and documents may be received in evidence without having a witness prove their accuracy. Included in this category are signed written statements of witnesses, containing facts and opinions that the witnesses would be allowed to testify to in person. Also included are other documents, such as hospital, medical or financial records (which were made in the ordinary course of business), bills, receipts and repair estimates.

In order to qualify under this rule, the statement or document must be served on all the parties at least 14 days prior to the trial date. The name and address of the author of the statement or document must be served at the same time. A party who has been served with such a statement or document then has the option of summoning the author to court as a witness. The party would do this if the statement or document appears to be damaging to his or her case and it seems likely that some of the damage could be undone by cross-examining the author on the witness stand.

If a party chooses to summon such a witness, he or she must notify all the other parties at the time that the summons is served. As well, the party summoning a witness will be responsible for witness costs, as outlined at the end of this chapter.

You should keep in mind, however, that the judge has the discretion to refuse to allow any statement or document to be admitted in evidence, even if the opposing party has accepted the evidence at face value and declined to summon the witness-author.

If you find yourself in this situation at trial, ask the judge for permission to call the author of the disputed statement or document as a witness. You may also wish to request an adjournment in order to arrange for the witness's attendance, but be prepared to argue with opposing parties about whether you should be responsible for any costs caused by the delay. You will argue that you fulfilled your obligations by serving opposing parties with the evidence as required by the rule.

If there are statements or documents you wish to use as evidence that require witnessing, you will need to call a witness or testify yourself in order to properly present your case. (See chapter 8 for information on how witnesses are used to introduce evidence at trial.)

b. HOW TO GET YOUR WITNESSES INTO COURT

There is only one way that you can be certain that the witness(es) you need to prove your case will show up in court, and that is by having them served with a summons (also known as a subpoena). You can obtain and fill out a summons at the court office (see Sample #15).

The summons will order them to appear at the trial and will contain the time, date and place of trial. It may also contain instructions to bring with them to court any books, papers or documents that are important to your case.

You will want to interview as many potential witnesses as possible in order to determine what information they have that may support your case. When talking to witnesses, don't prompt them, but simply ask them what they saw, heard and so on. This way you will get an accurate idea of what they will say on the witness stand if you call them.

SAMPLE #15
SUMMONS TO WITNESS

Provincial Court *(Civil Division)*
Cour provinciale *(Division civile)*
Toronto   Small Claims Court
.... *Cour des petites créances*

Ontario

Summons to Witness
Assignation

Form 19A
Formule 19A

Claim No /Demande n⁰
000/8-

Between/*Entre*

POLLY PLAINTIFF

Plaintiff/*Demandeur*

and/*et*

DESMOND DEFENDANT

Defendant/*Défendeur*

YOU ARE REQUIRED TO ATTEND TO GIVE EVIDENCE IN COURT at the trial of this action on (date)
VOUS ÊTES REQUIS(E) DE VOUS PRÉSENTER DEVANT LE TRIBUNAL POUR TÉMOIGNER lors du procès

November 15, 198-   , at (time) 10 a.m.   at (address of court)
de la présente action le (date)   , à (heure)   à/au (adresse du tribunal)

100 Justice Way, Toronto   and to remain until your attendance is no longer
                                et d'y demeurer jusqu'à ce que votre présence ne
required.
soit plus requise.

YOU ARE REQUIRED TO BRING WITH YOU and produce at the trial the following documents and things:
VOUS ÊTES REQUIS(E) D'APPORTER AVEC VOUS et de produire lors du procès les objets et documents suivants:

(State particular documents and things required)
(Indiquer les documents et les objets particuliers qui sont requis)   Photographs, notes

and all other documents relating to the action in your custody, possession or control.
ainsi que tous les autres documents pertinents à l'action et dont vous avez la garde, la possession ou le contrôle.

IF YOU FAIL TO ATTEND AS REQUIRED BY THIS SUMMONS, A WARRANT MAY BE ISSUED FOR YOUR
SI VOUS NE VOUS PRÉSENTEZ PAS COMME LE REQUIERT LA PRÉSENTE ASSIGNATION, UN MANDAT
ARREST.
D'ARRÊT PEUT ÊTRE DÉCERNÉ CONTRE VOUS.

October 25, 198-
(Date)

J. Clerke
(Signature of clerk/*signature du greffier*)

TO: (Name of witness)
DESTINATAIRE: *(nom du témoin)*   I. Witness
                                      321 Yonge Street
                                      Toronto, Ontario
                                      Z1P 0G0

75

The summons may be served by any person on the proposed witness personally or by leaving a copy of the subpoena at the usual place of residence of the witness. However, it is usually much more satisfactory to have the bailiff of the court serve your witness. Then you will have an independent witness to the fact that your proposed witness was in fact served.

Once a proposed witness has been served with the summons, the person who served that witness will swear an affidavit that he or she made the service or may swear before the judge orally that he or she so served the witness. This becomes important only if the witness does not appear at the trial, in which case the judge will want to be convinced that the witness was properly served before taking the serious step of issuing a warrant of committal (see below).

Persons such as police officers and other professional people do not like to be surprised by being served with a summons to appear at a trial if they have not been consulted in advance. It is often a good idea to discuss your problem with them before issuing a summons.

However, even in a case in which the witnesses are friends of yours, you should always serve them with summonses because it happens quite often that, on the day of the trial, the witnesses that you had fully expected to appear do not show up.

It should also be noted that summonses may be issued for witnesses of either the plaintiff *or* the defendant. However, it is often very difficult to learn who your opponent's witnesses are unless you have been served with proposed evidence or their identities have been disclosed in response to questions during a discovery or at trial.

Once a witness has been served with a summons, the witness must attend at court on the trial date and remain throughout the trial. If the trial is adjourned or not completed on the trial date, the witness must continue to attend on all further hearing dates until the trial has been completed or the witness dismissed. It is not necessary to serve the witness with another summons, but you should keep the witness informed of any future hearing dates that have been set.

A person who ignores a summons may be found guilty of contempt of court and be subject to a jail sentence.

If a witness who has been served with a summons fails to attend at court or leaves before he or she has been dismissed by the judge, the judge may issue a warrant. The warrant would empower police officers to apprehend the witness anywhere in Ontario and bring him or her before the court. Before taking such a measure, the judge would determine whether the witness's evidence was important enough to the proceedings to justify the issuance of a warrant.

If a witness is apprehended under a warrant, the witness may be detained in custody (jailed) until his or her presence is no longer required for the purpose of the trial. Alternatively, the judge may order the witness's release, but in so doing may order that the witness pay any costs arising out of his or her failure to come to or stay at court as required under the summons.

c. WITNESS COSTS

When deciding whether or not to summon witnesses, keep in mind the potential cost. You must pay a standard "conduct fee" to every witness you summon. The fee for a non-professional witness who need not travel far to court is under $10. The fee for a lawyer, doctor, engineer or veterinarian who testifies about his or her rendering of professional services is approximately $20. You will pay this sum directly to the court.

If you abuse your power to summon witnesses and summon a witness who clearly has no information to present to the court, then you may be ordered to compensate the witness for his or her inconvenience and expense in going to court unnecessarily. Such an order would not be made unless it was requested of the judge. (See Appendix 4 for a schedule of fees.)

8

THE TRIAL

This chapter describes in detail the rules and policies governing small claims court trial procedures. However, an invaluable way of acquainting yourself with what you can expect to happen at your trial is to attend at court beforehand and watch a trial or two.

a. WHAT TO DO WHEN YOU ARRIVE AT COURT

It is always a good idea to arrive at court a half-hour or so early. This will give you a chance to meet with your witnesses and discuss any last-minute matters that may have come up. If any of your witnesses have failed to arrive, you should telephone them in case they have forgotten.

Go to the courtroom named in your notice of trial. Check for the name of your case on the trial list posted outside the courtroom door. If no courtroom is named in the notice or your case does not appear on the trial list, go to the clerk's office and explain this. Your case may have been moved to a different courtroom.

The layout of courtrooms varies somewhat, but all are more or less as depicted in the diagram here.

When you enter the courtroom, you will take a seat in the public gallery until the name of your case is announced by the court clerk.

b. COURTROOM DECORUM

Before outlining the actual courtroom procedures, a preliminary note on court decorum is appropriate. You, and all your witnesses, should dress and conduct yourselves in a

DIAGRAM OF A COURTROOM

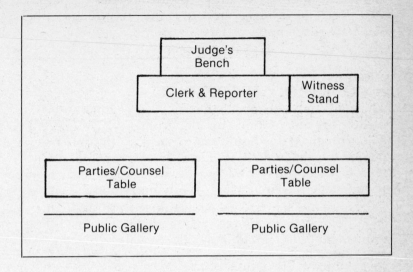

manner that shows your respect for the court. Whenever the judge enters or leaves the courtroom everyone present stands. Parties should never address the court from a sitting position. The judge should be spoken to directly and addressed as "Your Honor."

Generally, all court hearings are open to the public. However, if there is a possibility that this policy will result in serious harm or injustice to some person involved in the case, the court may order that the public be excluded. If the court makes such an order, it may also order that anyone who discloses information relating to the hearing will be subject to prosecution for contempt of court.

Generally, persons attending a court hearing are not allowed to take photographs of or tape-record the proceedings without the consent of the judge. Consent will not normally be given unless the purpose is educational and all of the parties and witnesses give their consent.

Contravention of this rule is an offence which is punishable by a fine of up to $10 000 or up to six months imprisonment or both.

People are allowed to *unobtrusively* make handwritten notes or sketches. Also, unrepresented parties are permitted to *unobtrusively* make a record of the proceedings, either by handwritten notes or tape-recording.

c. COURTROOM PROCEDURE

The judge normally opens the day's proceedings by asking if there are any motions for adjournment. If you need an adjournment, you should try to speak to the court clerk before the judge arrives. Then the clerk will announce your case and you will walk to the counsel table and explain to the judge the circumstances of your request.

If you have not had an opportunity to speak with the clerk beforehand, when the judge invites motions for adjournment, you should immediately walk to the counsel table and make your request. If you don't speak up at this point and other cases go ahead, you will have to wait until they have been dealt with. As discussed in chapter 6, only last-minute or contested adjournments will be sought at this time.

If an adjournment is granted, the party requesting the adjournment should send notice in writing to the other party indicating the new date for which the trial has been set.

Once the adjournments are dispensed with, the trial judge will begin to go through the day's trial list. You will recognize your own case by the name; for example, as in one of the cases used in the sample forms, the case would be referred to as No. 000/8- Polly Plaintiff vs. Desmond Defendant. You may have to wait for cases that are ahead of you to be heard.

When your case is called, the plaintiff and defendant should both walk to the counsel tables, introduce themselves to the court and then sit down.

At this time, the judge will ask if there are any preliminary motions to be made. In small claims court actions these usually arise only when the plaintiff has discovered that a mistake has been made in the statement of claim, which he or she would like to correct. The plaintiff will then ask the judge for permission to amend the claim. The defendant may well make objections if the amendment adversely affects his or her case. If the change is a major one, the judge may well refuse it. If the change is a minor one, but is sufficient to affect the position of the defendant in his or her defence, the judge may grant the amendment, but also grant an adjournment, so that the defendant can prepare a new defence based on the new claim, and will also award witness fees to the defendant for that day.

This problem can be avoided in many cases if the plaintiff has discovered the mistake a number of days before the trial. A notice of motion can be prepared and one copy sent to the small claims court and one copy to the defendant. See chapter 5 for more information on this. The clerk of the small claims court will be quite willing to assist you in preparing the form. If this is done, the defendant cannot object to your application on the grounds that he or she had no notice of it and that it interferes with the defence. The defendant may still argue that the proposed amendment is too substantial to be permitted at this late date, but this is something for the judge to decide.

d. IF YOU DON'T ATTEND

If none of the parties attends the trial, then the judge will simply strike the case off the trial list. If this happens and one of the parties wants the case to proceed to trial, he or she will have to bring a motion to have the case restored to the trial list.

If you are absolutely unable to attend the trial and you wish to have the trial date changed, see the discussion of adjournments above. Arrange to have someone go to court as your representative and explain why you cannot attend.

If at least one party attends, but one or more of the other parties do not, the trial judge has a choice:

(a) The judge may decide to go ahead with the trial anyway and the absent parties will probably be out of luck, unless they are later able to prove that they were not properly notified of the trial date.

(b) If the plaintiff attends, but the defendant does not, the judge may strike out the defence and, if there is a counterclaim, dismiss the counterclaim, and allow the plaintiff to go ahead and prove the amount of his or her claim.

(c) Similarly, if the defendant attends but the plaintiff does not, the judge may strike out the plaintiff's claim and dismiss the action and if the defendant has a counterclaim against the plaintiff, the defendant may be allowed to go ahead and prove the amount of the counterclaim.

(d) Finally, the court has the power to make any other order that is just. For example, if a party was unexpectedly unable to attend, but sent a representative to court to explain why and the judge was satisfied that the party had a very good reason for not attending, then an adjournment might be granted, probably together with an order that the party requiring the adjournment would compensate the other parties for the inconvenience and expense they had suffered as a result of wasting their time in court.

If a judgment is rendered in a party's absence, that party may apply to the court for an order to set aside or vary the judgment. If such an order is granted, costs may be awarded against the party who missed the trial. This will generally depend on whether the judge is convinced that the party had a satisfactory reason for being absent. See chapter 5 for information on how to bring a motion.

e. THIS IS IT — HOW TO HANDLE YOUR TRIAL

Following the preliminaries, the trial judge will direct the plaintiff to begin the case. The plaintiff should begin by giving the judge a very brief summary of the claim. The summary should not contain any of the evidence, but should simply state the nature of the claim. For example, in an action arising out of a contract, the plaintiff could simply say:

> Your Honor, this is an action on a contract between myself and the defendant in which I performed work for the defendant and she has not paid me.

It is also common practice for the plaintiff and the defendant in many actions, especially those arising out of automobile accidents, to agree on certain facts that are not in dispute. For example, in an automobile accident, they might agree upon the ownership of the automobile, the identity of the driver and, possibly, the amount of damages to the cars. This would leave the question of whose fault the accident was as the only issue before the court.

If such facts have been agreed upon, this would be the time for the plaintiff to state them to the court. Following the example above, the plaintiff might say:

> Your Honor, the defendant and I have agreed that there was such a contract and that it was made on July 31, 198-, and that the defendant was to pay me $300 upon completion of the work. The issue remaining between us is the question of whether or not I completed the work.

If you submitted an agreed statement of facts to the court before the trial, you should go over it briefly with the judge at this point.

If either party has witnesses present and there may be some difference between one person's version of the facts and another person's version of the facts, an order should be made at this point excluding these witnesses from the courtroom until it is time for them to take the stand. This will ensure that each witness will give independent testimony. This is done simply by asking the judge for an order for exclusion of witnesses and the judge will handle it from there.

At this time, the plaintiff will call the first witness who is usually himself or herself. After the plaintiff or the plaintiff's witness has presented his or her testimony, the defendant is entitled to cross-examine.

After the cross-examination by the defendant, the witness may be re-examined by the plaintiff. (Cross-examination and re-examination are discussed later in this chapter.)

After the plaintiff and all of his or her witnesses have given their evidence, the plaintiff will end his or her case and the defendant will then present his or her side of the case and call any witnesses he or she has. The same procedure of examination, cross-examination, and re-examination continues for each of the defendant's witnesses.

Throughout the trial, you should be making notes of witnesses' answers, so that you will be in a position at the close of the testimony to know what evidence has been heard by the judge. You will base your final argument to the judge on the evidence that has been favorable to you.

Remember those lists you made of facts you wanted to prove in court? This is the time to check off as many of them as you can, through your examination of your own witnesses and your cross-examination of your opponents'.

Another reason for staying alert is that your opponent may try to introduce evidence that is irrelevant and unfavorable. For example, you might be suing the defendant for a debt and the defendant might ask one of his or her witnesses, "Do you know that the plaintiff has a criminal record?" If something like this occurs, you should stand up as quickly as possible and say to the judge, "Your Honor, I object!"

Following the presentation of all the evidence, the judge will direct the plaintiff to begin the oral argument. When the plaintiff has finished, it will be the defendant's turn to present oral argument.

This simply means that each party will attempt to summarize the case in the best possible light. Further evidence may not be given at this time. Each party must refer in the argument to the evidence given in court by the witnesses, including any documentary evidence which may have been entered as exhibits. Each party stresses the facts he or she believes to be helpful to his or her side of the case.

After the oral argument has been completed, the judge will deliver his or her judgment. Usually this occurs immediately, but sometimes the judge reserves (postpones) the decision until a later date.

f. WHAT YOU SHOULD KNOW ABOUT THE RULES OF EVIDENCE

1. Admissibility

The rules of evidence are more loose in the small claims court than in the higher courts. The court may "admit" (accept) as evidence any testimony or document as long as it is relevant to the case. It does not matter whether or not the evidence has been proven under oath, but the court will have to be convinced that a document is authentic before it will be admitted.

However, if the court admits evidence that has not been proven in the usual way, it can decide not to give very much weight to that evidence. For example, the court might admit "hearsay evidence" (discussed below), but such second-hand information will be taken with a grain of salt.

A general rule of thumb is that whatever is relevant will be admitted and whatever is irrelevant will not. Evidence is relevant when it is directly related to the legal issues that the judge must resolve in order to determine whether a claim should succeed or fail.

Many volumes have been written on the law of evidence. Here, you are presented only with the basics. If you're unsure about the admissibility of any evidence you intend to present which is crucial to your case, get legal advice.

2. The rule against hearsay

The rule against hearsay is a fundamental rule of evidence and is designed to prevent witnesses from coming to court and telling the judge what they heard someone else say. Hearsay is an oral or written statement made by persons other than the witness who is testifying on the stand. It is not allowed in evidence if the purpose of putting it in evidence is to prove the truth of the facts contained in that statement. Thus, a plaintiff who intended to prove that the defendant in an automobile accident action drove through a red light would not be permitted to testify that he or she had heard another person state that the defendant had driven through the red light. If the plaintiff wants to get that evidence in, he or she must bring that other person to court to testify that he or she saw the defendant drive through the red light. In other words, the judge will take seriously first-hand observations only.

Many reasons are given for the exclusion of hearsay evidence, the most convincing being those that spring from the general requirement of our law that evidence must take the form of direct oral testimony given in public on oath and in circumstances where it can be tested by cross-examination. There are, however, some exceptions to this rule.

3. Exceptions to the rule against hearsay
The exceptions to the hearsay evidence rule are numerous and very complex. Many lawyers have difficulty understanding them. The most satisfactory method of dealing with the hearsay evidence rule is to remember that, generally speaking, you cannot testify in court to what someone else has said.

If you see another party or a witness of another party doing this, you may object to the judge who will determine whether or not to receive what is being put forth as evidence. It may be that there is some evidence that you wish to put into court and you are afraid that it might be hearsay. The best course you could take would be to consult a lawyer to determine the point. However, a few of the more common exceptions are included here to guide you.

Statements by a person who is a party to the trial can be introduced in evidence by another witness if those statements go against the interests of the party who made the statement. These statements could not be admitted into evidence if they went in favor of the person who made the statement. For example, if, after an accident, one of the plaintiff's witnesses heard the defendant say to another person, "The accident was my fault because I went through a red light," this could be introduced into evidence by the plaintiff's witness who heard it. However, if the defendant had said, "The accident is not my fault because I was driving carefully," this statement could not be introduced into the evidence by any witness.

The reason for this is said to be that it may safely be presumed that no person would declare anything against himself or herself unless it were true. There is no presumption of truth regarding statements in the speaker's own favor. If this were not so, every person could seek to improve his or her own position in pending or possible court actions by making statements in his or her own favor. However, once an admission against the speaker's interests is put into evidence, the whole statement must be put in and parts of it may well be favorable to the speaker.

It should be further noted that if the circumstances are such that the statement offered as an admission against interest was made in the course of an attempt to settle the dispute either before the action was commenced or while the action is going on, that statement is not admissible in evidence at all. This is because it is the policy of the law that disputes should be amicably settled, if possible, and it would discourage people from entering into negotiations if statements made during such negotiations were admissible in evidence at the trial if the attempt to settle is unsuccessful. For example, if you're suing for $500, you wouldn't want the judge to know that at some point you were willing to settle for $250.

Accordingly, anything that is said or written in the course of negotiations that are entered into expressly or by implication "without prejudice" cannot be given in evidence, even on a question of costs, without the consent of the party who made that statement. If the negotiations are by letter, lawyers often insert the words *without prejudice* at the head of the letter, although this is not necessary.

Another exception to the hearsay rule concerns statements contained in public or official documents that, subject to the qualifications below, are admissible as proof of the facts recorded. These statements and entries must have been made by the authorized agents of the public in the course of their duties, and the facts recorded must be of public interest or notoriety or must be required to be recorded for the benefit of the public. The principal documents of this description are statutes; parliamentary journals; gazettes; public registers and records; public inquisitions; surveys; assessments and reports; official certificates; corporation, company and bankers' books; and works of reference.

There are also a number of statements that would ordinarily be hearsay, but that are made admissible by the Canada Evidence Act or the Ontario Evidence Act. These include medical reports and books and records kept in the ordinary course of business by companies who normally keep such records.

There are, as stated earlier, numerous other exceptions to the hearsay rules, but those mentioned above are most likely to help you to introduce evidence in small claims court actions that might otherwise not be taken very seriously by the judge.

4. Direct examination and leading questions
When you want a witness to testify, you "call" the witness to the witness stand. Then the court clerk "swears in" the witness, asking him or her whether he or she promises to tell the truth.

After the witness has been sworn, it is the responsibility of the party who called the witness to examine him or her "in chief" or, as it is sometimes called, to conduct a "direct" examination. The object of the direct examination is to elicit from the witness all such information that tends to prove the party's case and that is within the personal knowledge of the witness.

These may be facts in issue or relevant to the issue and, in certain cases, hearsay or opinion. The hearsay should be avoided unless it fits into one of the exceptions, and the opinion can be given only if the person giving it is an expert in that field. All witnesses are considered experts when estimating the speed of an automobile, determining whether or not a person appears to be drunk, guessing a person's age, and other fairly ordinary tasks.

In order to have a witness give opinion evidence on specialized matters such as the extent of an injury or the cost of a car repair, you would have to call an expert witness with knowledge and experience in that particular area, such as medical doctor or a garage mechanic.

Generally speaking, a party may not, either in direct examination or re-examination elicit the facts of his or her case by means of "leading questions," that is, questions that suggest the desired answer or that put disputed matters to the witness in a form that will permit that witness to answer simply yes or no. For example, a person seeking to find out if the witness had seen the other party go through the red light should not ask, "Did you see Desmond Defendant drive through the red light?" Instead, the person should ask such questions as, "Did you see the vehicle approaching the intersection?"; "What was the color of the traffic light as the vehicle approached the intersection?" "What did the vehicle do upon reaching the intersection?" This, of course, assumes that the vehicle has already been identified as the one being driven by the other party.

And to introduce this evidence, you would not ask, "Was Desmond Defendant the driver of the car?", but instead, "Who was the driver of the car?"

The purpose of the rules against leading questions is to prevent the questioner from suggesting answers to the witness and, since the object is to prevent unfairness, the judge has a discretion to relax the rule whenever he or she considers it necessary in the interests of justice. It is always relaxed in proving introductory matters, such as the identification of the witness and the other preliminary matters. It is also relaxed when the party questioning the witness is seeking a direct contradiction of some previous testimony.

For example, if one party's witness has testified that it was raining and this is against your interest, you could ask your witness if it was raining or not, hoping to have testimony that it was not raining.

If parties were allowed to lead their witnesses freely though their evidence, there would be a great danger that the witnesses would tailor their stories to what the questioner wanted to hear, particularly since witnesses who are called by a party are usually sympathetic to that party's side of the dispute.

5. Cross-examination

Leading questions are permitted on cross-examination. Leading questions are a necessary tool in effective cross-examination of parties who are adverse in interest. The object of cross-examination is twofold:

(a) To weaken, qualify, or destroy the case of the opponent by either attacking the truthfulness of the witness or seeking to contradict or qualify the facts testified to in the examination-in-chief

(b) To establish the party's own case by means of the opponent's witnesses

Cross-examination is not confined to matters testified to in direct examination, but may embrace all relevant facts in issue, as well as those which, while otherwise irrelevant, tend to call into question the credibility of the witness.

Leading questions may also be put in, but the witness must not be misled by false assumptions or actual misstatements, and the judge has a discretion to disallow any question considered to be improper or oppressive.

Shouting at witnesses, asking the same question repeatedly, and arguing with witnesses is not permitted.

The credibility of a witness depends upon his or her knowledge of the facts, lack of interest in the result, integrity, and truthfulness. In order to test credibility, questions may be put to the witness in order to find out how the witness knows what he or she claims to know, what opportunity the witness had to make those observations, and what reasons the witness might have for giving the type of evidence he or she is giving.

Any relationship — whether family or business — between the witness and the party calling that witness may be discussed and, if denied, may be proven by other means.

Perhaps the most important types of questions are those reviewing the critical points of a witness's testimony in an attempt to expose errors, omissions, inconsistencies, or improbabilities. In cross-examining, you are free to suggest to the witness some alternative version of the facts he or she presented during direct examination and challenge the witness to deny your version.

Failure to cross-examine a witness will generally amount to acceptance of that witness's version of the transaction.

6. Re-examination

Whenever a party has conducted a cross-examination, the opposing party has the right to re-examine the same witness. However, this right is restricted to asking questions designed to explain matters that arose during the course of the cross-examination.

No new evidence may be introduced without the consent of the judge. The judge will tend to exclude any evidence that could have been introduced during the original examination of the witness.

For example, let's say you examine a witness about a part of a conversation the witness had that seems helpful to your case. Under cross-examination, the witness admits that he or she was distracted by something during this part of the conversation and therefore is unsure about what was said. If you wish to have the witness testify on some other part of the conversation in order to try to fix some of the damage that was done during the cross-examination, you will probably not be allowed to do so.

On the other hand, if the conversation came to light for the first time during the cross-examination and you had no way of knowing about it earlier, then you may be allowed to re-examine the witness about it.

The main thing to keep in mind is that your direct examination of each witness should be as complete as possible, so that you may avoid having to argue for your right of re-examination.

7. Documentary evidence

Generally speaking, documents, unless admitted by the other party, must be properly proven to be admissible. It is not normally sufficient to produce a document without proving its authenticity, unless by virtue of official character or for some other reason it comes within the class of documents that are admissible on mere production, or upon proof that it comes from proper custody.

An example of this type of document would be a certificate of a judgment in another court, a marriage licence or other type of official document. The original document, must, as a rule, be produced or its absence properly accounted for. But there are cases where copies are admissible even without accounting for the absence of the original. Examples of this are a certified extract of the registration of a particular vehicle received from the superintendent of motor vehicles proving the ownership of the vehicle or a deed proving ownership of land.

At this point it should be stressed that the person intending to prove documentary evidence is concerned with the proof of the execution of the document (that it was properly signed) as well as the proof of the contents of the document. It is essential to be able to establish both of these things. The law on these two points is fairly technical; however, if you intend to produce signed bills, receipts, promissory notes, etc., it is fairly simple to prove the validity of these documents by one of the following methods:

(a) The evidence of the writer
(b) The evidence of a witness who saw the document signed

(c) The evidence of a witness who has acquired a knowledge of the handwriting of the person you allege signed the document

(d) Comparison of the document in dispute with others proved to be genuine

(e) The admission of the party against whom the document was tendered

By far the most common method is to put the person who signed or witnessed the document on the stand.

To introduce the document, the examination would go something like this:

> **Question:** I am showing you a contract signed by two persons, one of whose name appears to be Desmond Defendant. Is that your signature, Mr. Defendant?
>
> **Answer:** Yes.
>
> **Question:** And is this the written version of the contract you made with Polly Plaintiff on June 23, 198-?
>
> **Answer:** Yes.
>
> **Question:** And is the other signature on this contract Ms. Plaintiff's?
>
> **Answer:** Yes, I saw her sign it.

It is necessary here to consider an important rule applicable only in small claims court. The judge may admit as evidence at a trial, whether or not it is proven under oath and whether or not it would be admissible as evidence in the Supreme Court of Ontario, any document or other thing relevant to the subject matter of the proceedings, and the judge may act on such evidence.

This rule does not permit the judge to admit as evidence a document that, under the rules of evidence, the other party is entitled to prevent from being admitted as evidence, or any document that is not permitted to be admitted at a trial by a statute. However, this rule otherwise alters the law of evidence, at the judge's discretion, to permit unproven documents to be considered by the court.

Finally, this rule permits a judge, where he or she is satisfied about its authenticity, to admit as evidence a copy of a document or other thing. An example of how this rule could be helpful is in the case of an automobile accident in which you submit your repair bill as evidence of the damage, without requiring the presence of the auto mechanic as a witness.

The most common examples of evidence governed by statute are business and medical records. Documents made in the course of business may be proved by calling as a witness any person who is familiar with the record-keeping of that business. You don't need to call the person who actually made the record. Payroll records are an example. Bank records, such as bank statements, fall under a similar rule.

A special rule applies to medical records. Even if you have chosen to call a doctor as a witness instead of using the procedure described in chapter 7, you must notify the other party at least seven days before the trial date that you intend to use a medical report as evidence and you must make a copy of the report available to them.

It may interest you to know that documentary evidence may include such items as photographs, sketches, diagrams, surveys and maps. But you may be required to call the photographer, etc., as a witness. If the item appears to be helpful and accurate, the judge will usually admit it.

Documents and other things that are admitted as evidence by the judge become "exhibits." They are numbered by the court clerk according to the order in which they are admitted.

8. Inspection of property

If questions arise during the trial concerning a particular place or property, the judge may decide to conduct an inspection of that place or property. A party might suggest to the judge that this should occur, or the judge might decide on his or her own that an inspection would assist in resolving the dispute (for example, in a case in which the quality of a renovation job is the matter in dispute).

Inspections of property such as damaged motor vehicles are unlikely to occur, because the damage can probably be shown by a photograph and an inspection would be a much more costly and time-consuming method of obtaining the same evidence.

If you are involved in one of the rare cases in which an inspection occurs, you should be sure to attend. All parties have the right to be present at or send representatives to any such inspection.

9. Use of evidence obtained on discovery
If a discovery has been held in your case, there are ways in which you may use admissions obtained during your examination of the other party.

Because it is so unlikely that discovery will be ordered, the rules regarding the admission of such evidence will not be dealt with here. If your case is so complicated as to justify the necessity of a discovery, you will probably require legal assistance.

g. THE JUDGMENT
The judgment is the decision made by the judge as to whether any party is liable to any other party and, if so, for how much money. A party may be awarded any amount by the judge up to the amount of damages claimed by the party.

If the damages being sued for continue to occur after the claim is made, the court will take into account the amount of damages suffered subsequent to the filing of the claim in determining the award of damages.

As an example, say you are the plaintiff and the case arose out of a cheque that was given to you by the defendant. The cheque, which was for $800 and was to repay you for a loan that you had made to the defendant, bounced. The defendant refused to pay you back, so you sued for your $800.

You filed your claim two months ago and the trial is coming up very soon. You realize that you have lost more than $800 as a result of the defendant's actions, because, in the meantime, you were unable to pay your rent and have been evicted by your landlord and put to the extra expense of moving and the inconvenience of locating a new apartment.

As another example, your claim might be for nuisance caused to you by a noisy neighbor. If you win at trial and you can show that your damages have increased since the time you filed your claim because the problem has continued since that time, you may be awarded damages for this subsequent interference with your enjoyment of your property.

The court may order a losing defendant to make payments on the judgment in instalments. As well, the court may reserve the right to review and change the award in the future. Defendants who are unable to "satisfy" (pay off) the judgment immediately should ask the judge to make an order for instalments.

Be prepared to give the judge a realistic assessment of how much and when you will be able to pay. If you fail to pay as ordered, the plaintiff may take a variety of actions against you, as discussed in chapter 9.

Whether or not any liability is found, the judge will have to decide who is to pay for the costs of the action and for what amount.

Generally, the court will order the unsuccessful party to pay for the disbursements of the successful party. Disbursements are legal expenses other than counsel fees. Examples are costs of filing and processing court documents, such as claims and summonses, as well as such items as photocopying, telephone calls and travel expenses.

The clerk will assess the amount of the disbursements of the successful party. However, the court will review the clerk's assessment and may arrive at a different figure. All amounts claimed must be reasonable and necessary for your preparation of your case. You should provide receipts where possible.

The court may also award a successful party up to $30 to be paid by the unsuccessful party to cover the costs of preparing for trial and filing the claim or defence, as the case may be.

Further, if a successful party who claimed or defended himself or herself against a claim of more than $500 was represented by a lawyer at the trial, the court may award up to $300, to be paid by the unsuccessful party toward the successful party's lawyer's fee. If the claim was for more than $500 and the successful party was represented by a law student, the court may order that the unsuccessful party pay up to $150 as a counsel fee.

If the claim was for more than $500 and the successful party represented himself or herself in court, and if the court is convinced that an unsuccessful party caused the trial to be unnecessarily complicated or lengthy, then the court may order that party to pay the successful party up to $300 as a compensation for his or her inconvenience and expense. This could include loss of income and travel costs. As well, there may be an order for costs to be paid to a witness who was unnecessarily summoned.

The judge must express his or her reasons for making the judgment. However, written reasons will not automatically be provided by a judge. If you wish to have written reasons, request this of the judge before he or she "delivers" (announces) the judgment. This is particularly important if you later wish to apply for a new trial and your case involves less than $500 in damages, because no official record of the proceedings in such case will be made.

The judge will normally hand down judgment immediately following the conclusion of the case. On rare occasions, the judge will "reserve" judgment which means he or she wants to think about it for a while. In this case, the judgment will be sent to the clerk of the small claims court who will then contact the parties. There is no requirement for the successful party to do anything to register, enter, or certify the judgment in any way. The staff at the office of the small claims court will do this automatically.

If the judge reserves judgment for more than six months, you should contact the chief judge of the small claims court. Such situations are extremely rare. If you find yourself in this situation, you might seek legal advice as to the possibility of obtaining permission from the chief judge for a new trial.

9

OVERTURNING THE JUDGMENT

If you have lost your case, you will probably want to consider one or more of the remedies discussed below. Time is of the essence in challenging any judgment and you should therefore assess your options as soon as judgment is rendered against you. Note the time limits given below.

Another reason to decide your course of action quickly is that the winner may take steps to begin collecting on the judgment as soon as it has been given. If this has occurred and you choose to use one of the procedures described below, you should make a motion to the court for a "stay" (halting) of enforcement proceedings.

a. GETTING A NEW TRIAL

Within 30 days after the trial, a party who is dissatisfied with the judgment may make a motion to the court for a new trial. (See chapter 5 for how to bring a motion.)

Retrials will be ordered only in unusual circumstances such as fresh evidence coming to light that was not available at the original trial. A common situation in which new trials are granted is when the defendant can show that he or she never received the claim and therefore lost the case by default. In this situation, the judge will usually set aside the default judgment on the condition that the defendant files a defence within 20 days.

In support of your motion for a new trial, you must provide the motions judge with the reasons for judgment given by the trial judge. In cases involving $500 or more, a court reporter will have been present at the trial. You may contact the reporter and order a transcript of the last part of the proceedings containing the judge's reasons.

In cases involving less than $500, no court reporter will have been present at the trial. Therefore, unless you made a tape-recording of the proceedings or requested the judge to issue written reasons to you, you will not have a record of the reasons, other than perhaps your own notes. If you're in this situation, you will simply state in your affidavit what you believe to be the trial judge's reasons for making his or her judgment.

Upon hearing the motion for retrial, the court has several options:

(a) It may dismiss the motion. If this occurs, the judgment that was handed down at the trial becomes final, unless an appeal is launched.

(b) It may substitute a different judgment from the one originally given. In other words, the judge could cancel an award given to one party and instead make an award to another party. Alternatively, the judge might vary the amount that was awarded to the successful party.

(c) It may grant the right to a new trial. If this occurs, a new trial date must be arranged. The trial takes place with the same parties and based on the same "pleadings" as in the original trial, unless a party wishes to add a party or change a claim or defence, in which case he or she may bring a motion for joinder or amendment, as the case may be. At the new trial, the parties may call new witnesses and introduce fresh evidence.

b. APPEALS

If you are unhappy with the judgment and believe that it was unfair or wrong, you may wish to appeal. An appeal is a request for a change in the judgment.

You may appeal from a judgment of the small claims court if the claim was for more than $500, or for the recovery of possession of personal property worth over $500. Appeals are heard by the divisional court, a branch of the Supreme Court of Ontario.

In most cases, you do not need permission from the divisional court in order to appeal. However, if you are appealing a decision that was reached with your consent or if your appeal is limited to a question of costs rather than damages, you will have to obtain permission from the divisional court to appeal.

If you have launched an appeal in divisional court, you may make motions to that court for "interim" matters. For example, if you have unsuccessfully brought a motion before the small claims court to stay enforcement proceedings against you, you may be able to convince the divisional court to stay the proceedings. (Enforcement is discussed in chapter 10.)

On the other hand, your opponent may bring a motion to "quash" (disallow) the appeal. This might occur if your opponent was able to convince the divisional court that you did not have grounds for your appeal.

In hearing appeals, the divisional court is empowered to receive new evidence and even to direct that a new trial take place. It will depend on the circumstances of the case. A new trial will not be ordered unless some substantial wrong or miscarriage of justice has taken place. Examples of this would be where the small claims court judge did not permit a party to make his or her final argument.

Your notice of appeal must be served within 30 days of the date of judgment and filed with the divisional court within 10 days of the date of service.

In addition, file a copy of your notice of appeal with the small claims court as soon as possible. Upon receipt of your notice, the small claims court will transfer your file to the divisional court. Your appeal cannot proceed until this has occurred.

Since the divisional court will not often disturb the decision of the trial judge in regard to the facts of the case, but will rather remain within the issues of the appropriate law involved in the case, it is almost essential that the appealing party be represented by a lawyer.

Cost is a very important consideration in appeals. Even if your lawyer's fees are covered by legal aid (see Appendix 1), you must be prepared to pay the legal costs of your opponent if you lose. In addition, the legal costs that must be borne by the appealing party are more substantial than those incurred at trial.

To sum up, before launching an appeal from a small claims court judgment, you should consider the following:

(a) Is the value of what is at stake more than $500?

(b) Do you have grounds for an appeal?

(c) If you're not eligible for legal aid, are you prepared to pay a substantial sum in court and legal fees?

(d) If you are unsuccessful in the appeal, are you able to pay much higher costs and legal fees to the other side?

In short, appealing is an expensive and risky business and deserves careful consideration before proceeding. When pride is involved, it is hard to think clearly. Therefore, it is always wise to let things settle down for a few days and consult a lawyer on the legal merits of an appeal in your case before deciding whether to go ahead with it.

It is also theoretically possible to appeal an order of the divisional court to the court of appeal (the highest court in Ontario) and from there go to the Supreme Court of Canada (the highest court in the country). Because such appeals occur so very rarely, they are not discussed here.

c. SETTING ASIDE DEFAULT JUDGMENT

If judgment has been rendered against you at the trial in your absence and you wish to have it overturned, you should bring a "motion to set aside default judgment" as soon as possible. (See chapter 5.) Be prepared to provide a very good reason for your failure to appear at the trial.

10

HOW TO COLLECT ON YOUR JUDGMENT

At this point, it should be made clear that the small claims court is not a collection agency. Many people think that, once judgment is handed down, the court will automatically collect the amount from the loser. Unfortunately this is not the case. The onus is on the winner to collect the judgment from the loser and, if the loser refuses to pay, to take execution (seizure and sale) and/or attachment (garnishment) proceedings, which are discussed below.

Once the judgment is handed down, the parties, for purposes of collecting the amount of the judgment, are called by different names. The successful party, who can be either the plaintiff or, where a counterclaim is involved, the defendant, becomes the creditor. The unsuccessful party becomes the debtor.

If both parties are successful, then they have each of the names in respect to the different judgments. That is, the plaintiff would become the creditor with regard to his or her successful claim, but the debtor with regard to the successful counterclaim of the defendant, and vice versa for the defendant.

In addition, a third party called the garnishee is often involved in collection proceedings. The garnishee's role is discussed below.

a. CHASING THE RELUCTANT DEBTOR
Once the creditor has obtained judgment, if it appears that the debtor is either hesitant or unable to pay, the following five remedies should be considered by the creditor:

(a) Garnishment of wages or bank account

103

(b) Execution (seizure and sale) against assets of the debtor

(c) Registering a writ of seizure and sale against any land held by the debtor

(d) Recovery of personal property through a writ of delivery

(e) "Examination" of the debtor in court

If the debtor is a corporation, the procedures in (a), (b), (c) and (d) are exactly the same as if the debtor were an individual. In addition, the remedy outlined in (e) is also valid against corporations, though the procedure is slightly different. Each of these remedies is explained in greater detail below.

The creditor may begin any of these enforcement procedures immediately after judgment is obtained, whether by default or at trial.

Debtors should keep in mind the general powers of the court to "stay" (put a temporary halt to) any collection proceedings and to vary the times and amounts of payments if the debtor can convince the court that his or her financial circumstances have changed.

For example, if a debtor becomes unemployed and the job was his or her only source of income, he or she would want to apply for a stay of any sale of property or other proceedings endangering his or her income that are scheduled. If the debtor lost his or her job and got another job that paid less, he or she might want to try to arrange with the court to reduce the amount or frequency of his or her payments to the creditor.

Also, a debtor who has more than one outstanding small claims court judgment against him or her may apply to the court for a "consolidation order." Such orders make it easier for the debtor to pay off the creditors. The procedure is discussed later in this chapter.

Debtors who plan to apply for a new trial or appeal the judgment should be aware that such action will not automatically put a stop to any enforcement proceedings creditors may take. The debtor will have to make a motion to the court for a stay of such proceedings.

Creditors should be aware that if the debtor plans to leave the province or take other measures to avoid paying the debt, there may be help available. Laws that may assist include the Absconding Debtors Act, the Fraudulent Debtors' Arrest Act and the Reciprocal Enforcement of Judgments Act. If you're a creditor in this situation, seek legal assistance.

Judgments are the most common type of order that people want enforced. For this reason, the discussion in this chapter refers to judgments only. However, any order of the small claims court may be enforced using the procedures described in this chapter. For example, garnishment, discussed below, could be used by a witness to collect his or her costs.

1. Garnishment

Garnishment is a procedure by which the creditor obtains a court order requiring an individual or corporation who owes the debtor some money to pay it to the court instead of to the debtor. The court then passes along the money to the creditor until the creditor's judgment has been satisfied.

Garnishment occurs primarily in the area of wages for employment, which would be owed by the debtor's employer to the debtor, although it can also be applied to such matters as bank accounts and other debts owing to the debtor.

In order to start garnishment procedures, you (as the creditor) need merely go to the offices of the small claims court in the territorial division in which the debtor resides and swear an affidavit that states —

(a) the date of the judgment and the amount of money awarded to you,

(b) the name of the territorial division in which the order was made,

(c) the rate of post-judgment interest payable to you,

(d) the date and amount of any payment received by you from the debtor since the judgment was handed down,

(e) the total amount owing to you, including the post-judgment interest,

(f) the name and address of each person to whom you wish to be sent a notice of garnishment,

(g) a statement that you believe that all of those persons are or will become indebted to the debtor and a statement by you as to what leads you to believe that this is so, and

(h) any information you may have about the details of these debts owed to the debtor by the persons you have named above.

You should have all of this information with you when you go to the court office; the staff can then assist you in filling out the affidavit, shown in Sample #16.

If the earlier proceedings that resulted in your getting judgment occurred in a territorial division other than the one in which the debtor resides (in other words, if you were earlier dealing with a different court office), you must also file a copy of the certificate of judgment. This will prove that you have obtained judgment and have the right to have it enforced.

You may obtain a certificate of judgment by paying a very small fee to the court office that handled your claim.

If you are dealing with the same court office in enforcing your judgment as you were in getting it, then you do not need to file the certificate of judgment, because the office will already have it on file.

Once you have filed the affidavit and, if necessary, the certificate of judgment, the clerk will issue a notice of garnishment to all of the persons named in your affidavit (see Sample #17).

In addition to providing the small claims court with the addresses of the proposed garnishees in the affidavit, the creditor must also provide the address of the debtor, so that all of these persons may be served by the court with the notices of garnishment.

In order to cover the costs of processing the necessary documents, you will be required to pay a small fee that you

SAMPLE #16
AFFIDAVIT FOR GARNISHMENT

Provincial Court *(Civil Division)*
Cour provinciale (Division civile)
Toronto   Small Claims Court
.... *Cour des petites créances*
Ontario

Affidavit for Garnishment
Serment de saisie-arrét

Claim No./*Demande n⁰*
000/8–

Between
Entre

POLLY PLAINTIFF

Creditor
Créancier

and
et

DESMOND DEFENDANT

Debtor
Débiteur

I, Polly Plaintiff   of the City of Toronto
Je,   *de la*
in the   Municipality   of Metropolitan Toronto   make oath and say:
du   *de*   *déclare sous serment:*
I am the above-named plaintiff (or the solicitor or agent for the plaintiff, as the case may be) in this action.
Je suis le demandeur susmentionné (ou l'avocat ou le mandataire du demandeur, selon le cas) dans cette action.
Judgment was recovered against the debtor, on   Tuesday   the 5th day of November   , 198– ,
J'ai obtenu jugement contre le débiteur le   *jour de*   , 19 ,
in the ....Toronto Small Claims Court....... as follows:
dans la   (name of court/*nom de la cour*)

Claim/*Demande*	$ 2 000.00
Costs/*Dépens*	$ 25.00
Prejudgment interest/*Intérêts antérieurs au jugement*	$ 40.00
Counsel fee/*Honoraires d'avocat*	$
Judgment/*Jugement*	$ 2 065.00
Additional costs/*Dépens supplémentaires*	$ 5.00
Postjudgment rate ( )/*Taux d'intérêt postérieur au jugement*	$ 50.00
Less payments received/*Moins les paiements perçus*	$ Nil
Total amount owing/*Montant total dû*	$ 2 120.00

I have reason to believe that ...Bigge Bank of Canada.............................
J'ai raison de croire que   (name of garnishee/*nom du tiers saisi*)

is indebted or will become indebted to the defendant for wages. If other than wages, give particulars.
*est ou sera redevable d'une rémunération au défendeur. S'il existe d'autres formes de titres de créance, en
donner la nature.* Money contained in a bank account of Mr. Defendant
The debtor resides at 11 Bay Street, Toronto Z1P 0G0
Le débiteur habite au

The garnishee resides or carries on business at
Le tiers saisi habite ou travaille au

SWORN BEFORE ME AT
REÇU A
this 15th day of January   A. D., 198– .
le

P. Plaintiff
Signature of Plaintiff, Solicitor or Agent
Demandeur, ou avocat ou mandataire du demandeur

J. M. Commissioner
A Commissioner for taking Affidavits
Commissaire aux serments

SAMPLE #17
NOTICE OF GARNISHMENT

Provincial Court (*Civil Division*)
Cour provinciale (*Division civile*)

Ontario

Form /Formule 21E

Refer to / Voir	**NO** 000	198-
Date of Judgment / Jugement rendu le	Nov. 15, 198-	
Court / Cour des petites creances	Toronto	
Unsatisfied / Montant impayé	$2 120	
Cost of Garnishee / Frais du tiers saisi		
Total	$	

Toronto .... SMALL CLAIMS COURT
COUR DES PETITES CRÉANCES DE
NOTICE OF GARNISHMENT/
AVIS DE SAISIE-ARRÊT

Between
Entre

POLLY PLAINTIFF

Creditor
Créancier

and
et

DESMOND DEFENDANT

Debtor
Débiteur

and
et

THE BANK OF TORONTO

Garnishee
Tiers saisi

A JUDGMENT of this court has ordered the debtor to pay a sum of money to the creditor. The creditor claims that you owe or will owe a debt to the debtor. The creditor has had this notice of garnishment directed to you in order to seize any debt that you owe or will owe to the debtor

UN JUGEMENT de ce tribunal a ordonné au débiteur de payer une somme d'argent au créancier. Le créancier prétend que vous êtes ou que vous serez redevable d'une dette au débiteur. Le créancier vous a fait adresser le présent avis de saisie-arrêt en vue de saisir la dette dont vous êtes ou serez redevable au débiteur.

YOU ARE REQUIRED TO PAY to the clerk of ..... TORONTO SMALL CLAIMS COURT ....
VOUS ÊTES REQUIS(E) DE PAYER AU GREFFIER DE

....

(name of court /nom du tribunal)

(a) within ten days after this notice is served on you, all debts now payable by you to the debtor; and

(b) within ten days after they become payable, all debts that become payable by you to the debtor within six months after this notice is served on you,

subject to the exemptions provided by section 7 of the *Wages Act.* The total amount of all your payments to the clerk is not to exceed

(a) dans les dix jours qui suivent la signification du présent avis, toutes les dettes dont vous êtes maintenant redevable au débiteur;

(b) dans les dix jours de leur exigibilité, toutes les dettes dont vous deviendrez redevable au débiteur dans les six mois qui suivent la signification du présent avis.

sous réserve des dispositions d'insaisissabilité prévues à l'article 7 de la Loi sur les salaires. Le montant total des paiements que vous ferez au greffier ne doit pas dépasser

$ ..... 2 120 ..... $

IF YOU DO NOT PAY THE TOTAL AMOUNT OR SUCH LESSER AMOUNT AS YOU ARE LIABLE TO PAY UNDER THIS NOTICE WITHIN TEN DAYS after this notice is served on you, you must file with the clerk a statement signed by you setting out the particulars

EACH PAYMENT MUST BE SENT to the clerk at the address shown below

IF YOU FAIL TO OBEY THIS NOTICE, THE COURT MAY MAKE AND ENFORCE AN ORDER AGAINST YOU for payment of the amount set out above and the costs of the creditor

IF YOU MAKE PAYMENT TO ANYONE OTHER THAN THE CLERK, YOU MAY BE LIABLE TO PAY AGAIN

SI VOUS NE PAYEZ PAS LE MONTANT TOTAL OU LE MONTANT INFÉRIEUR DONT VOUS ÊTES REDEVABLE EN VERTU DU PRÉSENT AVIS DANS LES DIX JOURS qui suivent sa signification, vous devez déposer auprès du greffier une déclaration signée de votre main dans laquelle vous apportez des précisions

CHAQUE PAIEMENT DOIT ÊTRE ENVOYÉ au greffier, à l'adresse indiquée ci-dessous.

SI VOUS NE RESPECTEZ PAS LE PRÉSENT AVIS, LE TRIBUNAL PEUT RENDRE ET FAIRE EXÉCUTER CONTRE VOUS UNE ORDONNANCE de paiement du montant précisé ci-dessus et des dépens du créancier.

SI VOUS PAYEZ UNE PERSONNE QUI N'EST PAS LE GREFFIER, VOUS POUVEZ ÊTRE TENU(E) DE PAYER DE NOUVEAU

TO THE CREDITOR, THE DEBTOR AND THE GARNISHEE *AU CRÉANCIER, AU DÉBITEUR ET AU TIERS SAISI*

Any party may request the court to determine any matter in relation to this notice of garnishment

Une partie peut demander au tribunal de statuer sur toute question relative au présent avis

(Date) (Signature of clerk, name and address of court signature du greffier, nom et adresse du tribunal)

Jan. 16, 198- J. Clerk Toronto Small Claims Court, 100 Justice Way, Toronto, Ontario may charge to the debtor by including it in the total owed by the debtor to you, as set out in your affidavit.

The notice of garnishment directs the garnishee to pay to the clerk of the court any money the garnishee owes to the debtor, up to the amount shown in the notice of garnishment. This money is to be paid within 10 days after the notice is received by the garnishee or, if the money is not owed to the debtor until a later date, within 10 days after that debt becomes payable. Debts are considered to be payable if they are to be paid by the garnishee to the debtor within six months after the notice is served.

If the garnishee is an employer of the debtor, the garnishee is only required to pay to the clerk 20% of the wages owed, up to the amount set out in the notice. This is because, under the Wages Act, 80% of employees' wages are protected from garnishment.

Creditors should be aware that it is not possible to garnishee the wages of civil servants in the ordinary way. If you wish to take garnishment proceedings against a civil servant, seek legal advice.

If the garnishee does not pay the clerk the amount set out in the notice of garnishment and also does not send the clerk a statement explaining why, the creditor may get an order against the garnishee for the amount in dispute. This is unless the court refused to award the creditor such an order during court proceedings to resolve the dispute about the garnishment money.

If a garnishee has received a notice of garnishment and pays the "attached" (garnisheed) money to someone other than the clerk of the court, the garnishee remains liable to pay that money to the clerk. On the other hand, any money paid by the garnishee to the clerk reduces the garnishee's liability toward the debtor.

For example, if the garnishee is an employer and is served with a notice of garnishment for $20, if he or she owes the debtor $100 in wages, then on paying the clerk $20, he or she owes only $80 more (80% of the total wage) to the debtor. "Wages" here means net wages, after income tax, Canada Pension Plan contributions and Unemployment Insurance premiums have been deducted.

If a garnishee wishes to dispute the garnishment or the amount of the garnishment, he or she is required to send a statement stating his or her reasons to the court within 10 days of receiving the notice of garnishment.

If there is no response to the direction to garnishee, the normal procedure is to telephone the garnishee and find out what the problem is. This is especially important if the garnishee is a large company, since they are notoriously slow in complying with these instructions. If the garnishee denies owing any money over the telephone or sends a statement to the clerk of the court saying that no money is owed to the debtor, you may accept this or you may request the clerk to put the matter on the trial list, to have the judge decide whether or not the garnishee should have paid any money into court.

If you choose to have the matter decided by the court, you will want to issue a summons to the garnishee to enable you to examine the garnishee properly at the hearing. The judge will normally assist you in examining the garnishee.

If the judge decides that there was a debt owing at that time, judgment will be entered against the garnishee in your favor. This might be your "big break," because usually the garnishee will be easier to collect from than the debtor. Should the judge decide that there was no debt owing at that time, you will be liable for the costs of the garnishee. *These costs are unlikely to be substantial, but keep in mind that they are not recoverable from the debtor.*

It may be that you will be partly successful in your attempt at garnishment in that some money is paid in, but not the whole amount. When this happens, you have the same alternative as you had when the garnishee failed to pay anything into court. Practically speaking, however, further action at this point is very rare, because in all likelihood the garnishee has acted properly in the matter. Since your garnishment was at least partially successful, the costs of this garnishment would be added to your costs that are recoverable from the debtor.

If the creditor, the debtor, a garnishee or any other "interested person" makes a request for a hearing, the court may resolve any disputes arising out of the garnishment proceedings. Interested persons might include other creditors who have somehow heard about the garnishment proceedings and wish to obtain the garnisheed funds for themselves.

Where it is alleged that the garnishee's debt to the debtor has been "assigned" or "encumbered" (see the Glossary), the court may order that the assignee or encumbrancer appear to answer questions about his or her claim to the disputed money. The court may decide who has the right to receive the money: the garnishee, the debtor and/or any assignee or encumbrancer.

The court may also vary or suspend periodic payments under a notice of garnishment. For example, if it was determined that the debtor requires 90% of his or her pay in order to support a dependent child or spouse, the court might decide to reduce the amount of the garnishee's payments from 20% to 10% of the debtor's pay cheque.

The judge will look at all of the financial circumstances of the debtor and the nature of the debt owed. Where appropriate, the judge may stay the garnishment proceedings.

Debtors who are financially strapped may bring a motion before the court for a hearing on the appropriateness of the garnishment. The clerk will send a notice to all parties giving the date of the hearing. If you want people who are not parties to attend, you will have to summon them as witnesses.

When the clerk receives a payment from a garnishee, he or she forwards the money to the creditor(s).

If you are not the only creditor seeking enforcement of a judgment against the debtor, the court will distribute any payments received from garnishees equally between all of the creditors who have filed requests for garnishment and have not yet been paid in full. However, if a hearing has been requested, the clerk will not distribute the money to the creditor(s) until the dispute has been resolved by the court.

As mentioned earlier, in addition to garnisheeing wages you may garnishee a debtor's bank account. In many cases, the debtor has not paid the creditor because he or she has no savings. But if the debtor has money in a bank account, it is available to the creditor through garnishment.

If you are lucky enough to know or be able to find out where the debtor banks, then there will be no problem in issuing a notice of garnishment. However, if you don't have this information, you may have to arrange for an examination of the debtor in order to find out.

When a bank receives a notice of garnishment, it will keep an eye on all accounts in the debtor's name. The accounts will be frozen for the garnisheed amount and whenever funds are deposited, they will be removed and forwarded to the court.

The debtor may have an account with the bank under a trade name or may have a joint account with someone else. The bank may freeze such accounts or may refuse to do so. If it refuses it will have to provide an explanation to the court and you will have an opportunity to dispute the freezing, as discussed above.

Any debt being garnisheed must be one that is owing to the debtor. If it is a joint debt owed to the debtor and someone else, it cannot be garnisheed, subject to the exception of joint bank accounts. In addition, there are a number of other situations in which there is an apparent debt, but it cannot be garnisheed.

For example, the debtor may be holding money or may be owed a debt in a capacity as a "trustee" for someone else. A trustee is one who holds property for the benefit of someone else, but has no real interest in it. A trustee cannot be garnisheed.

Thus you may have doubts about being able to garnishee a particular debt. Garnishee it anyway and put the onus on the garnishee to deny any liability. Frequently, garnishment attempts, even futile ones, put external pressures on the debtor to pay up. But remember that if your garnishment proceedings against a person are entirely unsuccessful, you will be liable to pay the costs that person incurred in disputing the garnishment.

Money paid into court by a garnishee is held for a couple of weeks in case the debtor wishes to bring a motion to have the garnishment set aside. Generally, the monies are mailed to the creditor twice per month.

2. Seizing personal assets

As an alternative to garnishment or in addition to it if it proves not to be entirely successful, the creditor should consider requesting the small claims court to issue a writ of execution against the goods of the debtor.

This simply means that the bailiff will go to the residence or other place where the debtor has goods and seize them. After seizing them, the bailiff must hold them until the interested parties and the public have been properly notified.

The court must notify the creditor and debtor at least 14 full days before the date when the bailiff intends to sell the property and an advertisement must also be published to bring the sale to the attention of prospective buyers. Then the sale will be held and the proceeds will be paid by the bailiff into court.

All that you as a creditor need to do to put the process into motion is go to the small claims court office in the territorial division where the debtor resides, give the clerk a written statement of the amount still owing and your name, address and telephone number, and request that a writ of seizure and sale of personal property be issued to the bailiff.

If you obtained your judgment in a different territorial division, you will have to provide the clerk with a copy of it.

You will need to give the bailiff the name and address of the debtor and any information you have concerning the debtor's assets, as this will greatly assist the bailiff in making a seizure.

You will have to pay a small fee to cover the bailiff's costs (see Appendix 4). This fee will be paid for out of any proceeds received from the sale of the debtor's goods. In addition, you will have to put down a deposit to cover the bailiff's costs in moving and storing the goods and holding the sale. The bailiff will tell you how much this charge will be.

The writ will remain effective for six months from the date it is issued and may be renewed for further six-month periods by filing a request with the clerk.

After the bailiff has seized the goods of the debtor, he or she must give a list of them to the debtor if he or she requests this.

After the goods have been seized, they are put up for sale at a public auction. Before the goods are sold, the debtor has the option of paying the clerk or bailiff the amount owing or so much of it as the creditor agrees to accept in full, together with the fees to repay to the bailiff. The writ may then be suspended.

If the debtor does not pay before the public auction, the sheriff will take the proceeds and put them into court. This money will be paid to the creditor. Any surplus of the sale of the goods is returned to the debtor after the deduction of all costs.

Seizure of goods is generally more useful against corporations than individuals, for several reasons. First, a number of personal goods are exempted from seizure under a writ of execution. For example, clothing of the debtor and his or her family is exempt up to a value of $1 000. Household goods and utensils are exempt from executions up to a value of $2 000. A worker's tools and other necessary implements for earning a living are exempt up to a value of $2 000. This includes an automobile, if the debtor needs it to earn a living, and is not merely a convenience. There are other exemptions and there are some exceptions to the exemptions which the bailiff is quite well aware of and will explain to you at the court office.

There is another drawback. Frequently the selling price of the goods after deducting the cost of seizure, cartage, storage, and selling the goods does not warrant the seizure.

Another important restriction on the usefulness of this method is the requirement that the debtor *own* the goods seized. Quite often, the goods in the possession of the debtor are subject to conditional sales contracts or chattel mortgages. This means the debtor does not have any "equity" in the goods. Also, it may be that the debtor owns goods jointly with a spouse or other person.

It is frequently difficult to know whether the debtor owns the goods. This is equally true whether the debtor is an individual or a corporation. Often a debtor has taken out one or more loans and put up his or her personal property as collateral. If this has occurred, it may be that a third party, such as a bank, owns the goods.

Unless this matter is investigated ahead of time, the debtor might produce papers at the time of seizure showing that the finance company really owns the seized goods and then the bailiff cannot take them.

It is possible to obtain this information, but the procedure is complicated and time-consuming. It will probably not be worthwhile for you to pursue this remedy unless the debt owed to you is substantial. If you wish to pursue this remedy, get legal advice.

3. Seizing land

If an order for the payment or recovery of money remains unsatisfied, the creditor is entitled to a writ of seizure and sale of any land owned by the debtor.

In order to obtain such a writ, the creditor simply files a written statement with the clerk of the amount owing by the debtor and, if necessary, a copy of the certificate of judgment. The clerk will then issue the writ of seizure and sale of land to a sheriff. (A sheriff is very much like a bailiff, but has more authority.)

However, if the order gives the debtor a certain amount of time to pay, the writ should not be issued until that time has expired.

Where the order that is being enforced calls for payment of the money owed by the debtor into court, the writ will specify that all money arising from any sale of the debtor's land by the sheriff must be paid into court.

Once a creditor has filed a writ of seizure and sale of land with a sheriff, the creditor may instruct the sheriff to enforce the writ by filing with the sheriff a "direction to enforce." The direction must include the following information:

(a) The date of the order and the amount awarded

(b) The rate of post-judgment interest payable (the court will tell you the rate)

(c) The costs of enforcement for which the creditor is entitled to be reimbursed by the debtor, such as fees for issuing, renewing and filing the writ (see Appendix 4)

(d) The date and amount of any payment received by the creditor from the debtor since the order was made

(e) The total amount owing, including post-judgment interest

The direction will also contain a statement by the creditor that he or she directs the sheriff to enforce the writ for the amount owing, further post-judgment interest, plus the sheriff's costs.

One disadvantage of the sale-of-land remedy is that the creditor is required to make a large deposit to cover the sheriff's expenses and protect him or her in case any unforeseen problems arise. The sheriff will tell you the amount required.

After a writ is filed, the creditor must wait for four months before taking any steps to have the land sold. After four months, if the creditor still has not been paid by the debtor and wishes to enforce the writ, certain advertising requirements must be met. The sheriff must mail notices of the time and place of the proposed sale to both the creditor and the debtor at least 30 days before the sale.

Additionally, the sheriff is required to advertise the sale widely ahead of time, so that all interested parties will have an opportunity to hear of the intended sale. Another reason for the advertising is that the more members of the general public who hear about the sale, the higher a price the sheriff is likely to get for the land.

Prior to any sale, the sheriff will, upon written request of the creditor, deliver to the registrar of land titles a copy of the writ. This creates a charge on the land owned by the debtor that might be registered in the land titles office. The registration with the sheriff covers any lands that the debtor might own and that are registered in the registry system. The effect of this is that the debtor cannot sell, mortgage, or in any way deal with the land without first paying the amount of the judgment registered against this land. Practically, it puts extreme pressure on the debtor to pay the debt.

If a creditor learns that a debtor has changed his or her name since the writ was issued, the creditor may file an affidavit describing the change and the sheriff will amend the writ by adding the new name. If the writ has been filed under the Land Titles Act, the sheriff will send a copy of the amended writ to the land registrar.

No sale of land subject to a writ of seizure and sale may be held until six months after the writ was filed with the sheriff.

One of the problems that may arise is that it may turn out that the debtor does not have much equity in the land. In other words, it may be that most of the value of the land or the building on it is taken up by mortgages, which have priority over writs filed against the land.

Another problem that may arise is that if a debtor has gone into bankruptcy and the court has appointed a receiver to manage the debtor's property, a writ may not be enforced against the property.

It is very important to seek legal advice before instructing the sheriff to sell any land under a writ.

If you are a debtor and are unhappy with the results of the sale, seek legal advice as to whether the sale was properly advertised by the sheriff.

The writ remains in force for six years from the time that it is issued, and it may be renewed for further six-year periods.

You may renew your writ by filing a "request to renew" with the sheriff *before the expiration date*. The court staff will assist you in making your request. The sheriff will make a note of the date of renewal on the writ.

A writ that has not been filed with the sheriff may be renewed *before it expires* by filing a "requisition to renew" with the clerk. The clerk will make a note of the date of renewal on the writ.

Once a writ is on file with the sheriff, he or she must warn the creditor between one and two months before the writ will expire. The creditor should receive a notice of expiration by mail.

4. Delivery of the creditor's personal property

An order for the delivery of personal property belonging to the creditor may be enforced by a "writ of delivery." The creditor must file an affidavit with the clerk stating that the property in question has not yet been returned. Then the clerk will issue the writ to the bailiff.

If the bailiff locates the property anywhere outside of a dwelling place, he or she is empowered to use a reasonable amount of force to enter the premises and "seize" (take possession of) the property. In order to seize property located in a dwelling place, the bailiff must first obtain a court order. If the bailiff is able to locate and seize the property, it will be turned over to the creditor-owner.

If the bailiff is unable to locate it, he or she will notify the creditor that this is the case. If this happens, the creditor has the option of making a motion to the court for an order that will allow the bailiff to seize other personal property of the debtor. If this occurs, the bailiff will hold the seized property until the court decides what will become of it.

b. EXAMINATION OF THE DEBTOR

As an alternative or in addition to any of the collection procedures outlined above, a creditor may have a debtor examined (questioned) by a judge. This route is particularly helpful in cases in which the creditor has very little information about the debtor's income and assets.

The creditor asks the clerk of the territorial division where the debtor either resides or carries on business to issue a notice of examination to the debtor (see Sample #18). The creditor must file an affidavit setting out —

(a) the date of the order and the amount awarded in the order,

(b) the name of the territorial division in which the order was made,

(c) the rate of post-judgment interest payable on the award (the court will tell you what the rate is),

(d) the date and amount of any payment received by the creditor from the debtor since the order was made, and

(e) the total amount owing by the debtor to the creditor (including post-judgment interest).

The staff at the court office will assist you in filling out and swearing the affidavit.

As in the case of applying for a notice of garnishment, if the order you are seeking to enforce was obtained in a different territorial division from the one in which you seek to have the debtor examined, you must also file a copy of your certificate of judgment.

The notice of examination must be served on the debtor at least 14 full days before the date of the examination. The court will serve the notice and arrange the examination date.

A small fee must be paid by the creditor to the court for processing these documents. (See Appendix 4.) Of course, you can charge this to the debtor.

The debtor may be examined regardless of whether the debtor is an individual or a business. If the debtor is a corporation, an officer or director of the corporation may be examined. Similarly, if the debtor is a partnership, a partner may be examined, and if the debtor is a sole proprietorship, the sole proprietor may be examined.

The court will need to have the name and address of this individual in order to effect service of the notice of examination. You will have obtained this information earlier by

SAMPLE #18
NOTICE OF EXAMINATION

 Provincial Court *(Civil Division)*
Cour provinciale *(Division civile)*
Toronto   Small Claims Court
Cour des petites créances de

NOTICE OF EXAMINATION
AVIS D'INTERROGATOIRE
Form / *Formule* 21F

Claim No. *Demande n⁰*
000/8-

Between / *Entre*

POLLY PLAINTIFF

Plaintiff / *Demandeur*

and / *et*

DESMOND DEFENDANT

Defendant / *Défendeur*

TO THE DEFENDANT:
AU DÉFENDEUR:

On / *Le* **November 15, 198-** the plaintiff recovered judgment against you in this court for
(date)   *le demandeur a obtenu un jugement contre vous devant ce tribunal.*

$ **2 000** and $ **25** costs. The judgment remains unsatisfied.

Ce jugement est de .... $ *et de* .... $ *au titre des dépens. Le jugement
demeure impayé.*

YOU ARE REQUIRED TO ATTEND AN EXAM-INATION to determine the means you have to satisfy this judgment and whether you intend to satisfy it or have any reason for not doing so.

VOUS ÊTES REQUIS(E) DE VOUS PRÉSENTER POUR ÊTRE INTERROGÉ(E) de façon que soient établis les moyens dont vous disposez pour acquitter ce jugement. Il sera également décidé si vous avez l'intention de l'acquitter ou si vous avez des motifs de ne pas le faire.

THE EXAMINATION WILL BE HELD at the next sittings of this court at ... **Toronto Courthouse**
L'INTERROGATOIRE AURA LIEU lors de la prochaine session de ce tribunal à/au

100 Justice Way, Toronto
(location of court/adresse du tribunal)

on / *le* **February 20, 198-** at / *à* **10 a.m.**
(date)   *(time/heure)*

TAKE NOTICE THAT IF YOU DO NOT APPEAR YOU MAY, BY ORDER OF THIS COURT, BE COM-MITTED TO A CORRECTIONAL INSTITUTION FOR UP TO FORTY DAYS.

PRENEZ NOTE QUE SI VOUS NE VOUS PRÉ-SENTEZ PAS, VOUS POUVEZ, PAR ORDONNANCE DE CE TRIBUNAL, ÊTRE INCARCÉRÉ(E) DANS UN ÉTABLISSEMENT CORRECTIONNEL PENDANT UNE PÉRIODE POUVANT ALLER JUSQU'À QUARANTE JOURS.

February 10, 198-
(Date)

J. Clerke
(Signature of clerk/Signature du greffier)

doing a corporate search (as explained in chapter 2) in order to provide the bailiff with the necessary information to serve the claim or counterclaim.

Witnesses who have information that the court must hear in order to conduct a thorough examination of the debtor's financial situation may also be required to attend the examination. You will have to summon them as explained in chapter 7.

At the examination, the debtor and any witnesses are questioned by the creditor and the judge. The questions will cover such matters as —

(a) the reason for the debtor's non-payment of the money awarded in the judgment,

(b) the debtor's income and property,

(c) any debts owed to or by the debtor,

(d) the disposal by the debtor of any property either before or after the order was made in favor of the creditor,

(e) the debtor's past, present and future means of satisfying the order, and

(f) whether the debtor intends to obey the order or has any reason for not doing so.

The creditor will want to ask such questions as "Are you employed?"; "Where?"; "How much are you paid?"; "What was your past employment?"; "Do you own any real estate?"; "Do you own a car?"; "What income do you receive besides wages?"; "Are you married?"; "Does your spouse work?"; "Do you have young children?"; "How many?"; "Do you have any bank (or trust company or credit union) accounts?"; "Where?"; "Do you have a safe deposit box?"; "What personal property do you own (furniture, television, jewelry, etc.)?"; "How much money are you carrying right now?"

If the debtor is a corporation, the judge will treat the matter as if an individual were being examined, with the exception that if the company has no assets, you cannot proceed further against the officer or director present. This is known as the principle of limited liability and is a major reason why people choose to incorporate their businesses.

If a corporation loses a court case, the corporation itself is the only party that is liable, not the people who work for or hold shares in the corporation. This means that only the assets of the corporation and not the personal assets of its directors or officers are available to satisfy a judgment.

This is one reason for being more careful when dealing with corporations. You may find out if a corporation is bankrupt by conducting a search. The procedure is rather complicated and you will need legal assistance.

Often, the judge is successful in obtaining some commitment from the debtor to pay the creditor. When the examination has been completed, the judge, with or without the debtor's consent, based on what he or she has heard, may order the debtor to pay the creditor.

If a debtor who has been served with a notice of examination does not attend the examination and the judge determines that the debtor deliberately decided not to show up, or if the debtor does attend, but refuses to answer questions properly asked of him or her, the judge may order that the debtor be sent to jail for up to 40 days.

If the judge makes this type of order, the clerk issues a "warrant of committal" to the bailiff, who is then entitled to take the debtor to jail. However, almost invariably, the judge orders the debtor to attend court to explain why the warrant should not be enforced, and once this type of order has been made, the bailiff is not allowed to arrest the debtor unless the court orders this at the later hearing.

Another notice of examination is served on the debtor, and debtors who failed to show up at the original examination hearing usually are persuaded by the prospect of incarceration to attend this one.

If you are a debtor, you should follow the instructions of the court that are given to you and, in that way, avoid incurring the extra penalty of contempt of court. Although a person is never sent to jail in Ontario for owing money, occasionally debtors have been sent to jail for contempt of court by disobeying a court order to appear.

At the later hearing, whether or not the debtor appears, the court may order that the warrant of committal be enforced, in which case the bailiff would take the debtor, if he or she could be located, to jail. Alternatively, the court may order the debtor to pay the creditor some amount of money or may order that the debtor attend a full-fledged examination hearing, most likely at a later date.

Once a warrant of committal has been issued, it remains effective for six months, and the court may renew it for a longer period. Presumably, however, only one period of incarceration may be ordered under each warrant of committal.

A debtor who is jailed must be released when the time ordered by the judge in the warrant of committal has passed, but the debtor may be released earlier if his or her release is ordered by the court.

c. CONSOLIDATION ORDERS

If a debtor has more than one unpaid judgment against him or her, the debtor may apply to the court for a "consolidation order." This sort of order makes it possible for the debtor to pay off all the judgments at once, a bit at a time.

While a consolidation order is in force, creditors may not take any enforcement proceedings against the debtor other than issuing a writ of seizure and sale of his or her land.

To obtain a consolidation order, the debtor must file a notice of motion stating that such an order is being sought.

The debtor must also file an affidavit setting out the following information:

- (a) The names and addresses of the creditors who have obtained an order against him or her
- (b) The amount owed to each creditor
- (c) The amount of the debtor's income from all sources and a description of each source of income
- (d) The debtor's current financial obligations and other information related to the debtor's ability to pay the

creditors, such as support required by dependants and bank or other loans

The affidavit is shown in Sample #19.

Copies of the notice of motion and affidavit must be served on each of the creditors named in the affidavit at least seven full days before the date of the hearing of the motion. The debtor will arrange the hearing date with the court.

During the hearing, the creditors may make suggestions to the judge as to what amounts and times of payment are appropriate, but the final decision will be the court's, presumably based on the debtor's ability to pay.

If the court decides to make a consolidation order, the order will describe the date, court, total amount and amount unpaid of each unsatisfied order, and the amounts and times of the payments to be made by the debtor to the court. (Of course, 80% of the debtor's income from employment will be protected by the Wages Act.) A sample consolidation order is shown in Sample #20.

If a consolidation order has been made and a new creditor obtains a judgment arising out of a debt that was owed *before* the consolidation order was made, the creditor may apply to be added to the order. This is done by filing a "certified" (official) copy of the judgment with the clerk. From then on the creditor shares in the payments made by the debtor under the consolidation order.

If a judgment is obtained against the debtor in regard to a debt that arose *after* the consolidation order was made, the consolidation order is cancelled.

It will also be cancelled if the debtor fails to make any payment within 21 days from when it is due under the order.

If the consolidation order is "terminated" (cancelled), the clerk notifies by mail all of the creditors named in the order. The debtor is not entitled to obtain another consolidation order for one year from the date of termination.

Any payments made by the debtor to the clerk under a consolidation order are put into a consolidation account.

SAMPLE #19
AFFIDAVIT IN SUPPORT OF APPLICATION
FOR A CONSOLIDATION ORDER

Provincial Court *(Civil Division)*
Cour provinciale (Division civile)
Toronto   Small Claims Court
....   *Cour des petites créances de*

Ontario

AFFIDAVIT IN SUPPORT OF APPLICATION FOR A CONSOLIDATION ORDER
AFFIDAVIT A L'APPUI D'UNE REQUETE EN VUE D'OBTENIR
UNE ORDONNANCE DE CONSOLIDATION

In the matter of an application for a Consolidation Order, by
Dans l'affaire d'une requête présentée en vue d'obtenir une ordonnance de consolidation par

Desmond Defendant   of/de 10 Easy Street   in the/dans le   City

of/de Toronto   in the/dans la Municipality   of/de Metropolitan Toronto

I/Je soussigné(e), Desmond Defendant

of the/de la   City   of/de   Toronto   in the/dans le Municipality

of/de Metropolitan Toronto
(occupation/profession)   , make oath and say/déclare sous serment:

1. That the following Judgments have been recovered against me in a Small Claims Court and the following amounts are still outstanding: / *Que les jugements suivants ont été rendus contre moi par une cour des petites créances et que les montants suivants restent encore impayés:*

Claim No. Demande N°	Court Cour	Creditor/Créancier	Amount of Judgment Montant du jugement	Amount Outstanding Montant impayé	Solicitor or Agent Procureur ou mandataire
000/8–	Toronto	Polly Plaintiff	$2 065.00	$2 120.00	---
000/8–	Sudbury	Jack Jones	$ 125.00	$ 60.00	---
000/8–	Wawa	Walter Smith	$ 675.00	$ 301.00	Laura Legal
000/8–	Cobourg	Pierre Winner	$1 000.00	$ 3.00	---

State number and relationship of persons wholly or partially dependent upon debtor If partial state relationship accurately

Here list any other relevant facts

2. That my income from all sources is as follows:/*Que mon revenu de toutes sources est le suivant:*
I earn $400.00 per week and I have four dependants: three children, all in school, and my wife, who was injured on the job and cannot work.

3. That I am/*Que je suis* a plumber
(occupation/profession)   presently employed by/*actuellement au service de*
at/à Plumbers Inc., 300 Lakeshore Road   in the/dans le   City

of/de Toronto   in the/dans la Municipality   of/de Metropolitan Toronto.

I pay $650 per month on a mortgage and make loan payments of $100 per month on a truck I purchased to carry on my business. My wife requires medical care that is not covered by O.H.I.P.

Indiquer le nombre et le lien de parenté des personnes totalement ou partiellement à la charge du débiteur. S'il s'agit de personnes partiellement à charge, indiquer avec précision le lien de parenté.

Enumérer ici les autres faits pertinents.

SWORN BEFORE ME AT   Toronto
REÇU A
this 15th day of February   A.D., 19 8– .
le

J. M. Commissioner
A Commissioner for taking Affidavits
Commissaire aux affidavits

Desmond Defendant
Signature

SAMPLE #20
CONSOLIDATION ORDER

Provincial Court *(Civil Division)*
Cour provinciale *(Division civile)*
Toronto .... Small Claims Court
Cour des petites créances de

Consolidation Order
Ordonnance de consolidation

Claim No./*Demande m*
000/8–

In the matter of an application for a Consolidation Order, by
Dans l'affaire de la requête en vue d'obtenir une ordonnance de consolidation, présentée par

Desmond Defendant   of 10 Easy Street   in the
     de   *dans le/la*

City   of Toronto   in the
     de   *dans le/la*

Municipality   of   Metropolitan Toronto
     de

Upon Application of   Desmond Defendant   Debtor, and upon reading the affidavit of
A la requête du débiteur   *, et à la lecture de l'affidavit souscrit et déposé par*

Desmond Defendant   , filed ~~and upon hearing the Solicitor(s) for the Debtor~~
     et après avoir entendu le(les) procureur(s) du débiteur

~~(and the Creditor or Creditors:)~~
(et du(des) créancier(s):)

IT IS ORDERED that the Debtor pay to the Clerk of the   Toronto   Small Claims Court on the
IL EST ENJOINT au débiteur de verser au greffier du/de la   *cour des petites créances, le*

Or as the case may be   day of each and every week
autre modalité de paiement   *jour de chaque semaine,*

commencing   Friday   , the 3rd day of March   A. D. 19 8–   the sum of
à partir du   19   *la somme de*

$ 100.00   to be distributed by the Clerk of the Court on an equal basis among the follow-
     $ que le greffier de la Cour doit répartir de façon égale entre les créanciers

ing Creditors of the Debtor, and such other Creditors as may file notice of their judgments with
suivants du débiteur, ainsi qu'aux autres créanciers qui auront déposé l'avis de leurs jugements

the Clerk of this Court, such payments to continue until the amounts outstanding on the Judgments
auprès du greffier de cette cour. Ces versements se poursuivent jusqu'à ce que les sommes échues

have been satisfied.
en vertu de ces jugements aient été recouvrées.

Here list Creditors under the above headings
Enumérer les créanciers aux rubriques ci dessus

Last procedure number numéro du dernier acte de procédure	Court cour	Creditor créancier	Amount of judgment montant du jugement	Amount outstanding montant échu	Solicitor or agent procureur ou mandataire
000/8–	Toronto	Polly Plaintiff	$2 065.00	$2 120.00	---
000/8–	Sudbury	Jack Jones	$ 125.00	$ 60.00	---
000/8–	Wawa	Walter Smith	$ 675.00	$ 301.00	Laura–Legal
000/8–	Cobourg	Pierre Winner	$1 000.00	$ 3.00	---

Dated at   Toronto   this 26th day of February   , 19 8– .
Fait à   *le*   , 19 .

Periodically, at least once every six months, the clerk distributes the money in equal shares to all of the creditors named in the order.

d. WHICH ENFORCEMENT PROCEDURE SHOULD YOU USE?

If you know the identity of the debtor's employer and/or where the debtor banks, you have hardly anything to lose by commencing garnishment proceedings.

If the debt owed to you is large and you know that the debtor owns property and garnishment has proved unsatisfactory, you should consider a writ of seizure and sale. However, as mentioned earlier, you must be prepared to invest some money and you will probably require legal assistance.

If you lack knowledge of the debtor's income, assets, and financial obligations to others, the debtor examination procedure has a good chance of paying off.

APPENDIX 1

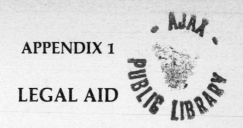

LEGAL AID

a. APPLYING FOR LEGAL AID

If you need a lawyer, but cannot afford to hire one and you qualify for legal aid, the Ontario Legal Aid Plan, which is funded by Ontario lawyers and the provincial and federal governments, will pay for all or part of your legal costs.

Any resident of Ontario may apply for legal aid. If your application is refused, you may request a review of the decision. If your application is approved, you will be given a legal aid certificate and may hire any lawyer who is willing to act for you. Approximately 70% of all lawyers practising in Ontario accept legal aid cases. See Appendix 2 for information on how to find a lawyer.

Your eligibility for legal aid depends on your financial situation and the nature of your case. When applying for legal aid, you should take with you to the legal aid office the following information:

(a) If you are employed, your pay slips (if you are married or living common-law, any pay slips of your "spouse")

(b) If you are unemployed, your separation certificate and/or proof of receipt of any unemployment insurance benefits

(c) If you are receiving welfare, your cheque stubs and/or drug card showing the amount of your benefits

(d) If you are self-employed, business statements and income tax returns

(e) If you are bankrupt, proof of receivership

(f) Up-to-date bank books/credit union statements

(g) A copy of your income tax return for the previous year, if possible

(h) A list of your income from all sources and assets, as well as expenses and debts

(i) Identification, such as your social insurance number or a driver's licence

It is an offence not to tell the truth about your financial situation.

You will also be required to describe your legal problem to the person who is processing your application.

In recent years, between 100 and 200 certificates per year have been granted in small claims court matters.

b. LEGAL AID OFFICES

Barrie
114 Worsley Avenue
L4M 1M1
(705) 737-3400

Belleville
150 Front Street
K8N 2Y7
(613) 962-9634

Brampton
11 Queen Street E.
L8W 2A7
(416) 459-6633

Brantford
111 Darling Street
N3T 2K8
(519) 759-4250

Brockville
32 Wall Street
K6V 4R9
(613) 342-5421

Chatham
48 Centre Street
N7M 4W2
(519) 352-1631

Cobourg
24 Covert Street
K9A 2L6
(416) 372-2432

Cornwall
139 Pitt Street
Suite 1
K6J 3P5
(613) 932-4756

Fort Frances
400 Scott Street
P9A 1H2
(807) 274-9571

Goderich
44 North Street
N7A 2T4
(519) 524-9612

Gravenhurst
195 Church Street N.
P0C 1G0
(705) 687-3700

Guelph
27 Douglas Street
N1H 2S7
(519) 824-0170

Hagersville
91 Main Street S.
N0A 1H0
(416) 768-1312

Hamilton
119 Main Street E.
L8N 3Z3
(416) 528-0134

Hawkesbury
102 Main Street E.
Suite 3
K6A 1A3
(613) 632-9009

Kenora
154 Main Street S.
P9N 1S9
(807) 468-6722

Kingston
295 Brock Street
K7L 1S5
(613) 546-1179

Kirkland Lake
12 Government Road W.
P2N 2E2
(705) 567-6696

Kitchener
133 Frederick Street
N2H 2M1
(519) 743-4306

Lindsay
22 Peel Street
K9V 3L8
(705) 324-6703

London
121 Queens Avenue
N6A 1H9
(519) 433-8179

Napanee
109 John Street
K7R 1R1
(613) 354-4773

Newmarket
50 Eagle Street
L3Y 1J3
(416) 888-1575

North Bay
215 Oak Street E.
P1B 8P8
(705) 472-4893

Oakville
225 Church Street
L6J 1N4
(416) 845-7591

Orangeville
70 First Street
Suite 10
L9W 2E5
(519) 941-4745

Oshawa
74 Simcoe Street S.
Suite 101
L1H 4G6
(416) 576-2124

Ottawa
167 Lisgar Street
K2P 0C3
(613) 238-7931

Owen Sound
945 Third Avenue E.
Suite 19
N4K 2K8
(519) 376-9130

Parry Sound
7 Miller Street
P2A 1S7
(705) 746-4011

Pembroke
17 Pembroke Street W.
K8A 5M4
(613) 732-4903

Perth
10 Market Square
K7H 1V7
(613) 267-3123

Peterborough
402 Water Street
K9H 3L9
(705) 743-5430

St. Catharines
183 King Street
L2R 3J5
(416) 685-1012

St. Thomas
16 Pearl Street
N5P 2N9
(519) 631-1190

Sarnia
546 North Christina Street
N7T 5W6
(519) 336-9371

Sault Ste. Marie
Court House
424 Queen Street E.
P6A 5M8
(705) 253-9401

Simcoe
71 Norfolk Street N.
N3Y 3N6
(519) 426-5780

Stratford
91 Brunswick Street
N5A 3L9
(519) 273-1050

Sudbury
144 Elm Street W.
P3C 1T7
(705) 673-8182

Thunder Bay
33 North Court Street
P7A 4T4
(807) 345-1972

Timmins
192 Third Avenue
P4N 1C8
(705) 264-9473

Toronto
70 Centre Avenue
M5G 2E7
(416) 598-0200

Walkerton
22 Jackson Street S.
N0G 2V0
(519) 881-0407

Welland
80 King Street
L3B 3J2
(416) 735-1559

Windsor
42 Pitt Street W.
Second Floor
N9A 5L4
(519) 255-7822

Woodstock
524 Dundas Street
N4S 1C5
(519) 539-2381

APPENDIX 2

ADDITIONAL SOURCES OF FREE OR INEXPENSIVE LEGAL ADVICE

Free legal advice is available to people with a modest level of income and assets. Call the clinic nearest you for advice as to whether you come within the guidelines set by the Ontario Legal Aid Program.

a. LAWYER REFERRAL SERVICE

If you do not qualify for free advice, the clinic may refer you to lawyers who charge a relatively small fee. Also, you can obtain a half-hour legal consultation with a lawyer experienced in the area you are interested in for $20 from the Lawyer Referral Service. To obtain the name of a lawyer in your area participating in this service, telephone the Law Society at 947-3330 in Toronto; call 1-800-268-8326 (toll-free) from most other areas of the province; and from most of area code 807, ask the operator for Zenith 5-8600.

Tell the person who takes your call what type of advice you require and he or she will give you the name of a lawyer who is willing to offer the half-hour consultation. Over 6 000 lawyers participate in this program, and many are experienced in civil litigation.

b. DIAL-A-LAW

You may also wish to contact Dial-a-Law. From Metro Toronto, dial 947-3333; from area code 416, dial 1-800-387-2920 (toll-free); from area codes 519, 613 and 705, dial 1-800-387-2992 (toll-free); and from most of area code 807, ask the operator for Zenith 99210.

Give the person who answers the phone a brief description of your problem. He or she will assist you in determining the exact type of legal advice you require and will then play a tape-recording giving a short lecture on that topic. Over 100 tapes are available covering 13 major areas of law. Several tapes deal with the small claims court and others deal with such topics as collection of debts, deceptive trade practices, purchasing defective goods, unsatisfactory services, and how to find a lawyer.

Both the Lawyer Referral Service and Dial-a-Law are services offered free to the public by the Law Society of Upper Canada, the institution responsible for regulating the legal profession in Ontario.

c. OTHER SOURCES OF ADVICE

Community Legal Education Ontario (listed below) sells pamphlets on a variety of legal topics. You may also check the list of titles in the Self-Counsel Series provided at the back of this book for books that deal with your particular legal problem.

d. COMMUNITY LEGAL CLINICS

Community legal clinics provide free legal services to persons with relatively minor legal problems who cannot afford to hire a lawyer. They are staffed by lawyers, community legal workers ("paralegals") and law students, and are funded by the government. Some clinics offer general legal assistance, while others specialize in a particular area of law, as indicated by the names of the clinics in the list below.

Advocacy Resource Centre for the Handicapped
Suite 255
40 Orchard View Boulevard
Toronto, M4R 1B9
(416) 482-8255

Algoma Community Legal Clinic
Suite 503
123 March Street
Sault Ste. Marie, P6A 2Z5
(705) 942-4900

Bloor Information and Legal Services
835 Bloor Street W.
Toronto, M6G 1M1
(416) 531-4613

Canadian Environmental Law Association
Fourth Floor
243 Queen Street W.
Toronto, M5V 1Z4
(416) 977-2410

Central Toronto Community Legal Clinic
364 Bathurst Street
Toronto, M5T 2S6
(416) 363-0304

Centre for Spanish-Speaking Peoples
582A College Street
Toronto, M6G 1B3
(416) 533-0680

Clinique juridique populaire de Prescott-Russell
577 McGill Street
Hawkesbury, K6A 2S2
(613) 632-1136

Community Legal Education Ontario
62 Noble Street
Toronto, M6K 2C9
(416) 530-1800

Community Legal Services
(Ottawa-Carleton)

71 Daly Street
Ottawa, K1N 6E3
(613) 238-7008

Community Legal Services of Niagara South
27 Division Street
P.O. Box 128
Welland, L3B 3Z5
(416) 732-2447

Crystal Beach Satellite Office
(416) 894-4775
Toll-free from Welland:
382-2536

Dundurn Community Legal Services
426 Main Street W.
Hamilton, L8P 1K6
(416) 527-4572

Durham Legal Clinic
Third Floor
40 King Street W.
Oshawa, L1H 1A4
(416) 728-7321

East Toronto Community Legal Services
930 Queen Street E.
Toronto, M4M 1J5
(416) 461-8102

Flemingdon Community Legal Services
Suite 110
747 Don Mills Road
Don Mills, M3C 1T2
(416) 424-1965/1984

**Halton Hills Community
Legal Clinic**
5 Wesleyan Street
Georgetown, L7G 2E2
(416) 877-5256
(519) 853-2400

**Hastings & Prince Edward
Legal Services**
194 Front Street
Belleville, K8N 2Y7
(613) 966-8686

**Industrial Accident
Victims Group of Ontario**
Suite 304
845 St. Clair Avenue W.
Toronto, M6C 1C3
(416) 651-5650/5686

**Injured Workers'
Consultants**
Suite 402
815 Pape Avenue
Toronto, M4J 1L2
(416) 461-2411

**Jane Finch Community
Legal Services**
Suite 201
1977 Finch Avenue W.
Downsview, M3N 2V3
(416) 746-3334

Justice for Children
Suite 105
720 Spadina Avenue
Toronto, M5S 2T9
(416) 920-1633

**Keewaytinok Native
Legal Services**
Box 218
Moosonee, P0L 1Y0
(705) 336-2981

**Kenora Community
Legal Clinic**
336 Second Street S.
Kenora, P9N 1G5
(807) 468-8888

Kinna-aweya Legal Clinic
233 Van Norman Street
Thunder Bay, P7A 4B6
(807) 344-2478

**Landlord's Self Help
Centre**
110 Atlantic Avenue
Toronto, M6K 1X9
(416) 532-4467

Legal Assistance Kent
78 Wellington Street W.
Chatham, N7M 5K1
(519) 351-6771

**Legal Assistance
of Windsor**
85 Pitt Street E.
Windsor, N9A 2V3
(519) 256-7831

London Legal Clinic
121 Queen's Avenue
London, N6A 1H9
(519) 679-6771

**McQuesten Legal and
Community Services**
360 Queenston Road
Hamilton, L8K 1H9
(416) 545-0442

**Metro Tenants
Legal Services**
Suite 233
366 Adelaide Street E.
Toronto, M5A 3X9
(416) 364-1486/1487

**Mississauga Community
Legal Services**
30 Stavebank Road N.
Mississauga, L5G 2T5
(416) 274-8531

**Neighborhood
Legal Services**
238 Carlton Street
Toronto, M5A 2L1
(416) 961-2625/2673

**Niagara North
Community Legal
Assistance**
8 Church Street
St. Catharines, L2R 3B3
(416) 682-6635

**North Frontenac
Community Services
Corp.**
P.O. Box 250
Sharbot Lake, K0H 2P0
(613) 279-2223/2928

**Parkdale Community
Legal Services**
1239 Queen Street W.
Toronto, M6K 1L5
(416) 531-2411

**Renfrew County
Legal Services**
Suite 3
180 Plaunt Street S.
Renfrew, K7V 4H2
(613) 432-8146

**Rexdale Community
Information and
Legal Services**
1530 Albion Road
Rexdale, M9V 1B4
(416) 741-1553

Rural Legal Services
c/o Faculty of Law
Macdonald Hall
Queen's University
Kingston, K7L 3N6
(613) 547-5860

**Scarborough Community
Legal Services**
Suite 9
695 Markham Road
Scarborough, M1H 2A4
(416) 438-7182

**Simcoe Legal Services
Clinic**
43 West Street N.
Orillia, L3V 5C1
(705) 326-6444

Sioux Lookout Community Legal Clinic
56 Front Street
Sioux Lookout, P0V 2T0
(807) 737-3074/3075

Stormount, Dundas and Glengarry Community Legal Clinic
4 Montreal Road
Cornwall, K6H 1B1
(613) 932-2703/2706

Sudbury Community Legal Clinic
215 Elm Street W.
Sudbury, P3C 1T8
(705) 674-3200

Tenant Hotline
1215 St. Clair Avenue W.
Toronto, M6E 1B5
(416) 656-5500

Waterloo Region Community Legal Services
30 Francis Street S.
Kitchener, N2G 2A1
(519) 743-0254
Cambridge area
(519) 653-1640

West End Legal Services
2835 Dumaurier Avenue
Ottawa, K2B 7W3
(613) 596-1641

York Community Services
1651 Keele Street
Toronto, M6M 3W2
(416) 653-5400

e. STUDENT LEGAL AID SOCIETIES

The following law schools offer the legal services of law students under the supervision of lawyers.

Osgoode Hall Law School
Community Legal Aid
Services Program
York University
4700 Keele Street
Downsview, M3J 2R5
(416) 667-3143

Queen's University
Queen's Law Students'
Legal Aid Society
Macdonald Hall
Kingston, K7L 3N6
(613) 547-2694

University of Ottawa
University of Ottawa
Student Legal Aid Society
105 Copernicus Street
Ottawa, K1N 7K6
(613) 231-3311

University of Toronto
Downtown Legal Services
84 Queen's Park Crescent
Toronto, M5S 1A1
(416) 978-6497

University of Western Ontario
Community Legal Services
Faculty of Law
Room 120
London, N6A 3K7
(519) 679-2818

University of Windsor
Community Legal Aid
Faculty of Law
Windsor, N9B 3P4
(519) 253-4232

f. DUTY COUNSEL

The following offices offer the services of publicly funded lawyers one day a week, as indicated. Telephone the office ahead of time to make an appointment, except in the case of the Warden Woods Community Centre, which accepts clients on a first-come first-serve basis only.

Action Service Contact Centre
185-5th Street
Toronto, M8V 2Z5
(416) 255-5322
Monday: 1:30 p.m. —
7:30 p.m.

Cedarbrae District Library
545 Markham Road
Scarborough, M6G 2L6
(416) 431-2222
Wednesday: 6:30 p.m. —
8:00 p.m.

Dixon Hall
58 Sumach Street
Toronto, M5A 3J7
(416) 863-0499
Tuesday: 6:30 p.m. —
8:30 p.m.

Humber College Lakeshore 1 Campus
Students Administrative
Council Office
3199 Lakeshore
Boulevard W.
Toronto, M8V 1K8
(416) 252-5571 ext. 3287
Monday: 1:00 p.m. —
4:00 p.m.

**Neighbourhood
Information Centre**
91 Barrington Avenue
Toronto, M4C 4Y9
(416) 698-1626
Tuesday: 6:00 p.m. —
8:30 p.m.

**Warden Woods
Community Centre**
74 Firvalley Court
Scarborough, M1L 1N9
Thursday: 7:00 p.m. —
9:00 p.m.

**West Central Etobicoke
Community Relations**
Bloordale Community
School
10 Toledo Road
Etobicoke, M9C 2H3
(416) 626-4229
Wednesday: from 6:00 p.m.

APPENDIX 3

SMALL CLAIMS COURT OFFICES

Alexandria Small Claims Court
21 Harrison Street
P.O. Box 1551
Alexandria, K0C 1A0
(613) 525-1872

Alliston Small Claims Court
46 Centre Street
P.O. Box 706
Alliston, L0M 1A0
(705) 435-9645

Amherstburg Small Claims Court
1389 Front Road S.
Amherstburg, N9V 2M5
(519) 736-2667

Bancroft Small Claims Court
R.R. #4
Bancroft, K0L 1C0
(613) 332-4613

Barrie Small Claims Court
Court House
114 Worsley Street
Barrie, L4M 3P2
(705) 728-4181

Beardmore Small Claims Court
55 Pearl Street
P.O. Box 90
Beardmore, P0T 1G0
(807) 875-2222

Belleville Small Claims Court
123 Front Street
Belleville, K8N 2Y6
(613) 962-2300

Bracebridge Small Claims Court
Court House
P.O. Box 1821
Bracebridge, P0B 1C0
(705) 645-2682

Brampton Small Claims Court
Court House
7765 Hurontario Street
Brampton, L6V 2M7
(416) 451-0121

Brantford Small Claims Court
34 Market Street
Brantford, N3T 2Z5
(519) 753-0451

Brighton Small Claims Court
76 Young Street
P.O. Box 97
Brighton, K0K 1H0
(613) 475-0961

Brockville Small Claims Court
27 King Street E.
Brockville, K6V 1A7
(613) 342-2833

Burlington Small Claims Court
548 Locust Street
P.O. Box 384
Burlington, L7R 3Y3
(416) 632-0680

Cambridge Small Claims Court
120 Main Street
Cambridge, N1R 1V7
(519) 623-0170

Carleton Place Small Claims Court
205 Mailey Drive
Carleton Place, K7C 3V3
(613) 257-5124

Cayuga Small Claims Court
County Court House
55 Munsee Street
P.O. Box 58
Cayuga, N0A 1E0
(416) 772-3403

Chapleau Small Claims Court
21 Young Street
P.O. Box 584
Chapleau, P0M 1K0
(705) 864-0712

Chatham Small Claims Court
21 Seventh Street
P.O. Box 205
Chatham, N7M 5K3
(519) 354-0210

Cobourg Small Claims Court
208 Division Street
P.O. Box 546
Cobourg, K9A 4L3
(416) 372-7153

Cochrane Small Claims Court
149 Fourth Avenue
P.O. Box 1688
Cochrane, P0L 1C0
(705) 272-4151

Collingwood Small Claims Court
649 Hurontario Street
Collingwood, L9Y 2N6
(705) 445-4240

Cornwall Small Claims Court
340 Pitt Street
P.O. Box 1294
Cornwall, K6J 5B2
(613) 932-1224

Dryden Small Claims Court
Room 127
Ontario Government
Building
P.O. Box 636
Dryden, P8N 2Z3
(807) 223-2613

Durham Small Claims Court
P.O. Box 103
Durham, N0G 1R0
(519) 369-3505

Elliot Lake Small Claims Court
12 Gillanders Road
Elliot Lake, P5A 1W3
(705) 848-2383

Englehart Small Claims Court
16-6th Avenue
Englehart, P0J 1H0
(705) 544-2598

Espanola Small Claims Court
Town Hall
100 Tudhope Street
P.O. Box 126
Espanola, P0P 1C0
(705) 869-1150

Etobicoke Small Claims Court
2265 Keele Street
Suite 209
Etobicoke, M6M 5B8
(416) 249-8251

Fergus Small Claims Court
208 St. Andrew Street W.
Fergus, N1M 1N7
(519) 843-1644

Forest Small Claims Court
1 James Street
P.O. Box 327
Forest, N0N 1J0
(519) 786-5329

Fort Frances Small Claims Court
333 Church Street
P.O. Box 8
Fort Frances, P9A 3M5
(807) 274-5961

Geraldton Small Claims Court
624 Main Street
P.O. Box 39
Geraldton, P0T 1M0
(807) 854-1488

Goderich Small Claims Court
61 Hamilton Street
P.O. Box 512
Goderich, N7A 1R1
(519) 524-7112

Gore Bay Small Claims Court
Court House
Phipps Street
Gore Bay, P0P 1H0
(705) 282-2461

Grimsby Small Claims Court
31 Baker Road N.
P.O. Box 293
Grimsby, L3M 2W9
(416) 945-2756

Guelph Small Claims Court
25 Douglas Street
Guelph, N1H 2S7
(519) 822-0131

Haileybury Small Claims Court
Court House
Main Street
P.O. Box 1360
Haileybury, P0J 1K0
(705) 672-3606

Haliburton Small Claims Court
Highland Street
P.O. Box 209
Haliburton, K0M 1S0
(705) 457-1732

Hamilton Small Claims Court
P.O. Box 680
Hamilton, L8N 3M6
(416) 522-9063

Hawkesbury Small Claims Court
464 Laurier Street
Hawkesbury, K6A 2A6
(613) 632-4282

Huntsville Small Claims Court
578 Brunel Road
P.O. Box 2592
Huntsville, P0A 1K0
(705) 789-5630

Iroquois Small Claims Court
320 Church Street
P.O. Box 70
Iroquois, K0E 1K0
(613) 652-2173

Iroquois Falls Small Claims Court
885 Centennial Street
P.O. Box 369
Iroquois Falls, P0K 1G0
(705) 232-4374

Kaladar Small Claims Court
Highway 41
P.O. Box 51
Kaladar, K0H 1Z0
(613) 336-8952

Kapuskasing Small Claims Court
22 Hill Street
P.O. Box 182
Kapuskasing, P5N 2Y3
(705) 335-6383

Kenora Small Claims Court
216 Water Street
Kenora, P9N 1S4
(807) 468-6270

Killaloe Station Small Claims Court
Court House
King Street
Killaloe Station, K0J 2A0
(613) 757-2050

Kingston Small Claims Court
County Court House
Court Street
Kingston, K7L 4X6
(613) 547-2231

Kingsville Small Claims Court
17 Division Street S.
Kingsville, N9Y 2E8
(519) 733-2633

Kirkland Lake Small Claims Court
29A Duncan Avenue
P.O. Box 217
Kirkland Lake, P2N 3H7
(705) 567-7060

Kitchener Small Claims Court
58 Scott Street
Kitchener, N2H 2R1
(519) 745-8063

Lindsay Small Claims Court
59 Victoria Avenue N.
Lindsay, K9V 4G4
(705) 324-4251

Listowel Small Claims Court
595 Inkerman Street E.
Listowel, N4W 2N8
(519) 291-1423

Little Current Small Claims Court
15 Robinson Street
P.O. Box 363
Little Current, P0P 1K0
(705) 368-2277

London Small Claims Court
80 Dundas Street
P.O. Box 5600
Terminal "A"
London, N6A 1E7
(519) 679-7017

Marathon Small Claims Court
17 Birch Street
P.O. Box 224
Marathon, P0T 2E0
(807) 229-1383

Marmora Small Claims Court
108 Forsyth Street
P.O. Box 158
Marmora, K0K 2M0
(613) 472-2501

Meaford Small Claims Court
Highway 26

P.O. Box 742
Meaford, N0H 1Y0
(519) 538-3618

**Milton Small Claims
Court**
Court House
491 Steeles Avenue E.
Milton, L9T 1Y7
(416) 878-6771

**Mississauga Small Claims
Court**
470 Hensall Circle
Mississauga, L5A 3V5
(416) 277-1583

**Mount Forest Small
Claims Court**
178 Main Street N.
P.O. Box 329
Mount Forest, N0G 2L0
(519) 323-4358

**Napanee Small Claims
Court**
35 Dundas Street E.
P.O. Box 51
Napanee, K7R 3L8
(613) 354-5243

**Newmarket Small Claims
Court**
Court House
50 Eagle Street
Newmarket, L3Y 6B1
(416) 895-4291

**Niagara Falls Small
Claims Court**
5415 Victoria Avenue
Suite 4
Niagara Falls, L2G 3L1
(416) 356-3404

**Nipigon Small Claims
Court**
4 Front Street
P.O. Box 309
Nipigon, P0T 2J0
(807) 887-3829

**North Bay Small Claims
Court**
390 Plouffe Street
North Bay, P1B 4G1
(705) 472-5860

**North York Small Claims
Court**
47 Sheppard Avenue E.
2nd Floor
North York, M2N 5X5
(416) 225-4846

**Oakville Small Claims
Court**
297 Lakeshore Road E.
Suite 4
Oakville, L6J 1J3
(416) 845-7941

**Orangeville Small Claims
Court**
21 First Street
Orangeville, L9W 2C8
(519) 941-1392

Orillia Small Claims Court
104 Borland Street E.
Orillia, L3V 6J6
(705) 326-4251

Oshawa Small Claims Court
14½ King Street E.
Oshawa, L1H 2L5
(416) 723-9332

Ottawa Small Claims Court
56 Sparks Street
Room 206
Ottawa, K1P 5Z4
(613) 232-5408

Owen Sound Small Claims Court
880 Second Avenue E.
Owen Sound, N4K 2H3
(519) 376-6659

Parry Sound Small Claims Court
89 James Street
Parry Sound, P2A 1T7
(705) 746-5464

Pembroke Small Claims Court
Court House
297 Pembroke Street E.
Pembroke, K8A 3K2
(613) 732-2541

Perth Small Claims Court
43 Drummond Street
Perth, K7H 1G1
(613) 267-2021

Peterborough Small Claims Court
Court House
Peterborough, K9H 3M3
(705) 745-0583

Picton Small Claims Court
9 Queen Street
Picton, K0K 2T0
(613) 476-2390

Port Elgin Small Claims Court
607 Mill Street
P.O. Box 1621
Port Elgin, N0H 2C0
(519) 832-2253

Port Hope Small Claims Court
3 Jane Street
Port Hope, L1A 2E4
(416) 885-8695

Prescott Small Claims Court
146 King Street W.
P.O. Box 1270
Prescott, K0E 1T0
(613) 925-4633

Red Lake Small Claims Court
Government Building
Howey Street
P.O. Box 226
Red Lake, P0V 2M0
(807) 727-2767

Renfrew Small Claims Court
898 Raglan Street S.
P.O. Box 386
Renfrew, K7V 4A6
(613) 432-3193

Richmond Hill Small Claims Court
550 Major MacKenzie Drive
Richmond Hill, L4C 4X7
(416) 884-3833

Rockland Small Claims Court
2560 Lalonde Street
P.O. Box 250
Rockland, K0A 3A0
(613) 446-4781

St. Catharines Small Claims Court
59 Church Street
2nd Floor
P.O. Box 574
St. Catharines, L2R 6W8
(416) 682-1560

St. Thomas Small Claims Court
2 Wellington Street
St. Thomas, N5R 2P2
(519) 631-1241

Sarnia Small Claims Court
180½ North Christina Street
Sarnia, N7T 5T9
(519) 337-6651

Sault Ste. Marie Small Claims Court
Court House
424-440 Queen Street E.
Sault Ste. Marie, P6A 1Z7
(705) 253-5141

Scarborough Small Claims Court
2130 Lawrence Avenue E.
Suite 300
Scarborough, M1R 5B9
(416) 755-5228

Schreiber Small Claims Court
105 Ontario Street
P.O. Box 234
Schreiber, P0T 2S0
(807) 824-2495

Sharbot Lake Small Claims Court
General Delivery
Sharbot Lake, K0H 2P0
(613) 279-2537

Shelburne Small Claims Court
R.R. #1
Shelburne, L0N 1S0
(519) 925-5040

Simcoe Small Claims Court
Court House
P.O. Box 605
Simcoe, N3Y 4N4
(519) 426-3447

South River Small Claims Court
440 Ottawa Avenue E.
P.O. Box 239
South River, P0A 1X0
(705) 386-2560

Stratford Small Claims Court
Court House
1 Huron Street
Stratford, N5A 5S4
(519) 271-4940

Strathroy Small Claims Court
52 Frank Street
Strathroy, N7G 1B9
(519) 245-1477

Sturgeon Falls Small Claims Court
Old Town Hall
Holtditch Street
P.O. Box 416
Sturgeon Falls, P0H 2G0
(705) 753-1090

Sudbury Small Claims Court
38 Larch Street
Sudbury, P3E 5M7
(705) 675-4164

Sutton West Small Claims Court
151 High Street
P.O. Box 7
Sutton West, L0E 1R0
(416) 722-5118

Thessalon Small Claims Court
14 Maple Street
Thessalon, P0R 1L0
(705) 842-3220

Thunder Bay Small Claims Court
Court House
277 Camelot Street
Thunder Bay, P7A 4B3
(807) 344-5801

Timmins Small Claims Court
47 Pine Street S.
Timmins, P4N 2J9
(705) 264-3808

Toronto Small Claims Court
444 Yonge Street
2nd Floor
Toronto, M5B 2H4
(416) 598-2842/2843

Trenton Small Claims Court
80 Division Street
Trenton, K8V 5S5
(613) 392-1655

Uxbridge Small Claims Court
8 Brock Street W.
P.O. Box 340
Uxbridge, L0C 1K0
(416) 852-7113

Walkerton Small Claims Court
Court House
215 Cayley Street
P.O. Box 430
Walkerton, N0G 2V0
(519) 881-0211

Wallaceburg Small Claims Court
437 James Street
Wallaceburg, N8A 2N8
(519) 627-1174

Wawa Small Claims Court
42 Superior Avenue
Wawa, P0S 1K0
(705) 856-7079

Welland Small Claims Court
102 Main Street E.
P.O. Box 612
Welland, L3B 5R4
(416) 734-7417

Whitby Small Claims Court
306 Dundas Street W.
2nd Floor
P.O. Box 386
Whitby, L1N 5S4
(416) 668-3624

Wiarton Small Claims Court
507 Mary Street
P.O. Box 514
Wiarton, N0H 2T0
(519) 534-1714

Winchester Small Claims Court
461 Gladstone Street
P.O. Box 13
Winchester, K0C 2K0
(613) 774-3374

Windsor Small Claims Court
744 Ouellette Avenue
Windsor, N9A 1C3
(519) 258-8751

Woodstock Small Claims Court
461 Dundas Street
Woodstock, N4S 1C2
(519) 537-8511

APPENDIX 4

SMALL CLAIMS COURT FEES

The following rates are valid as at June 15, 1985. The fees are usually increased annually by a small amount. Check with your local court office for current rates.

a. CLERK'S FEES

1. Upon filing a claim, third-party claim or counter-claim —

(a) (i) Where claim does not exceed $100		$6.60
(ii) Where claim exceeds $100 but does not exceed $500		$12.10
(iii) Where claim exceeds $500 but does not exceed $1 000		$17.60
(iv) Where claim exceeds $1 000		$23.15
(b) Where there is more than one defendant in an action, for each additional defendant		$2.20
(c) For every original action entered, to cover postage and handling		$4.40
(d) For each new or subsequent address on a service		$2.20

2.

(a) Receiving documents from another court
office for service $1.55

(b) Postage and handling   <u>$0.60</u>

3. $2.15

(a) Transmitting documents to another court
office for service $1.05

(b) Postage and handling   <u>$0.55</u>

     $1.60

4.		Receiving and entering a claim transferred from another court office on a judge's order	$2.20
5.		Filing a notice of motion (except a notice of motion under the Wages Act)	$10.00
6.			
	(a)	Issuing a summons to witness	$1.10
	(b)	Every additional copy	$0.50
7.			
	(a)	Preparing certificate of judgment for transmission to another court office	$2.10
	(b)	Postage and handling	$0.60
			$2.70
8.		Receiving certificate of judgment	$1.10
9.		Receiving for enforcement a process from a provincial court or an order of judgment, as provided by a statute	$11.00
10.		Issuing a writ of delivery	$5.50
11.		Issuing a writ of seizure and sale	$5.50
12.			
	(a)	Issuing a notice of garnishment	$8.50
	(b)	Fee to be deducted from each payment into court made under a notice of garnishment	$8.50
	(c)	Placing garnishee proceeding on the trial list	$2.20
13.		Preparing and filing consolidation order	$44.10
14.		In the distribution of funds collected under a consolidation order —	
	(a)	5% of funds received for distribution to be charged to the debtor, and	
	(b)	5% of amount to be distributed and actual cost of postage to be charged to creditors	
15.		Issuing notice of examination	$6.60
16.		Issuing warrant of committal	$3.30

17.	Forwarding court file to divisional court for appeal	$1.10
18.	Certified copy of judgment	$1.10
19.	If registered mail is necessary for transmitting a document, the full cost of postage shall be paid as an additional fee.	
20.	Search by a person not a party to the action	$1.10
21.	Preparing a copy of a document	$1.10
22.	Preparation of records of orders — per name	$0.25
23.	Referee services —	
(a)	Preparing notices of pre-trial hearings, lists of matters to be heard by referee, other related matters, per claim	$2.70
(b)	Postage and handling	$0.55
		$3.25

b. BAILIFF'S FEES

1.

   (a) For service of a claim or third-party claim $6.60

   (b) Postage and handling, one fee only $0.65

   (c) In addition to the fee payable under sub-item (a), where there is more than one defendant a fee of $6.60 shall be paid for each additional defendant

2.

   (a) For each kilometre necessarily travelled, except in an unsuccessful attempt to effect service, the kilometre allowance set out in Ontario Regulation 283/82, subject to item 3.

   (b) For each unsuccessful attempt to effect service $1.10

3.

   (a) In the territorial divisions referred to in sub-item (b), for each attempt to effect

service, whether successful or unsuccessful —

   (i)   If the bailiff necessarily travels more
          than 16 km, the travel allowance set
          out in Ontario Regulation 283/82,

   (ii)   In all other cases   **$1.10**

(b) Sub-item (a) applies to the territorial di-
     visions known as —

          Hamilton Small Claims Court
          Ottawa Small Claims Court
          Toronto Small Claims Court
          Etobicoke Small Claims Court
          Scarborough Small Claims Court
          North York Small Claims Court

4.   Service of summons to witness   **$2.20**

5.   Service of notice of garnishment on garni-
      shee   **$2.20**

6.   Service of notice of garnishment on debtor   **$2.20**

7.   Service of notice of examination   **$4.40**

8.   Enforcing a writ of delivery or a writ of
      seizure and sale of personal property   **$6.60**

9.   Preparing inventory of personal property
      seized under a writ of seizure and sale   **$6.60**

10.   Advertising sale of personal property
      seized under a writ of seizure and sale   **$1.10**

11.   Reasonable allowance and disbursements
      necessarily incurred to remove property
      seized, and for assistance in the seizure, or
      to secure or retain property, including
      appraisers' fees, if necessary

12.   If the order for the payment of money is
      satisfied in whole or in part after seizure
      and before sale, 5% of the amount directed
      to be enforced or 5% of the value of the
      property seized, whichever is less

13.   Enforcing warrant of committal   **$11.00**

c. WITNESSES' FEES AND ALLOWANCES

1. For attendance in court, unless item 2. applies, per day $6.00

2. Barristers, solicitors, physicians, surgeons, engineers and veterinary surgeons who are not parties to the action and who attend to give evidence of a professional service rendered by them or to give a professional opinion, per day $15.00

3. Reasonable travelling expenses actually incurred, but not exceeding the kilometre allowance set out in Ontario Regulation 283/82

d. COUNSEL'S FEES

A person who hires a lawyer and agrees to pay a certain rate is obligated to pay that rate regardless of whether the case is won or lost (or settled or discontinued). Usually there is an hourly rate to cover preparation for court, paperwork, etc., and a fixed per diem for the court appearance. But the most a winning party can get from the other party for "costs" (*legal* costs) is set out on pages 96 and 97.

APPENDIX 5

LAWS GOVERNING THE SMALL CLAIMS COURT

Both the following documents may be obtained at the Ontario Government Bookstore, 880 Bay Street (at Grosvenor) in Toronto ((416) 965-3088) for a few dollars.

- Courts of Justice Act, 1984
  Statutes of Ontario 1984, Chapter 11
- Rules of the Provincial Court (Civil Division)
  Ontario Regulation 797/84, amended by O. Reg. 158/85

Other relevant regulations include:

- Designated Courts — Bilingual Proceedings, O. Reg. 806/84
- Duties of Clerks and Bailiffs of the Provincial Court (Civil Division), O. Reg. 796/84
- Rules of Civil Procedure, O. Reg. 560/84, am. 786/84
- Territorial Divisions and Court Office Locations for the Provincial Court (Civil Division), O. Reg. 159/85

GLOSSARY OF LEGAL TERMS

Terms in quotation marks are defined elsewhere in the Glossary.

ABANDONMENT
(see Discontinuance)

ABSENTEE
A person whose whereabouts are completely unknown.

ACTION
To put it simply, a lawsuit. Actions involve civil law, whereas prosecutions involve criminal law.

ADJOURNMENT
The postponing of an action until another specified time or indefinitely, in which case it is called an adjournment *sine die*. When an adjournment is made peremptory, this means that the parties must appear on the trial date or lose their right to participate in the action.

ADMISSIBILITY
Testimony, documents and other things which by law may be accepted by a judge in his or her consideration of a legal dispute are said to be admissible as "evidence." The main requirement for admissibility is relevance.

ADMISSIONS
Confessions, concessions, or voluntary acknowledgments of fault made by a party in relation to a matter in dispute; statements made by a party or someone identified with that party of the existence of a fact or facts which are relevant and beneficial to the party's opponent.

ADVOCATE
One who argues a cause in an attempt to persuade a decision-maker.

AFFIDAVIT
A written (typed or handwritten) document stating facts that are sworn to be true by the person signing it. It is sworn before someone having the authority to administer an oath. Such persons include lawyers, notaries public and commissioners. Some staff members of the small claims court are commissioners.

AGENT
A person who represents a party in court.

ALLEGATION
Something that is claimed to have been said or done, but hasn't yet been proven in court.

APPEAL
An attempt by the loser at trial to have the judgment reversed.

APPLICATION
(see Motion)

ARGUMENT
The expression of a point of view about how a legal principle should be applied to the facts of a particular case. After all witnesses have testified at a trial, each party has the opportunity to make an argument to the judge.

ASSESSMENT
An examination by a court official of the amount of counsel fees and disbursements claimed by a winning party to ensure that they are reasonable (formerly called "taxation of costs").

ASSIGNEE
(see Assignment)

ASSIGNMENT
The transfer of rights under a contract to another person. This is normally done by finance companies and other institutions giving credit. The person who assigns the rights is called the assignor and the person to whom they are transferred is the assignee.

ASSIGNOR
(see Assignment)

ATTORNEY-GENERAL
The chief legal officer for the province.

BAILIFF
An officer of the court responsible for serving certain court documents, seizing and selling property under writs and arresting persons under warrants.

BANKRUPTCY
The state of being unable to meet financial obligations. Generally speaking, once a person becomes bankrupt, all debts acquired prior to the bankruptcy are discharged.

BREACH OF CONTRACT
(see Contract)

CAPACITY
Legal recognition of the ability of a person to sue someone or defend himself or herself in court.

CAUSE OF ACTION
The legal right to sue someone. In small claims courts, causes of action are based on "torts."

CERTIFIED COPY
A copy of a public document, such as a deed or a municipal by-law which is stamped and signed as a "true copy" by a public official. Certified copies are often "admissible" as "evidence," without having to call the author of the document as a witness.

CHARGE
In the land titles system of land registration, this is the equivalent of a "mortgage."

CHATTEL
(see Personal Property)

CIVIL LAW
(see Civil Litigation)

CIVIL LITIGATION
This encompasses all "actions" in the area of civil law. Civil law encompasses all disputes between individuals based on the law of "torts."

CLAIM
A statement of facts by a "plaintiff" as to why he or she is entitled to the "judgment" requested. The claim also serves as the official notification to the defendant that he or she is being sued.

CLERK
The clerk most often referred to in this book works in the court office and is responsible for such matters as issuing claims and notices, noting defaults and explaining the rules of the court to its users. There are also court clerks who assist judges in handling the administrative aspects of cases, such as taking witnesses' oaths and keeping track of "exhibit" numbers.

COLLATERAL
Property rights pledged by a borrower to a lender in return for being given a loan. If the borrower defaults on the loan, the lender may take over the property rights. By taking collateral, the lender secures his or her investment. For example, if you want a bank loan, you might be required to pledge your car as collateral. You will continue to be able to use the car, unless you fail to make your loan payments as required.

COMMISSION EVIDENCE
Testimony that has been given before a "special examiner," and recorded and transcribed. In rare cases, where a witness is unavailable to attend a court, this evidence may be used instead of live testimony.

COMMITTAL ORDER
An order made by a judge that a "warrant of committal" is to be enforced.

CONSENT
Permission of a party. It is always best to get it in writing. If all parties agree to a certain outcome, then the judge will make an "order" on consent.

CONTEMPT OF COURT
Disobeying a court order and other flagrant displays of disrespect for the court. This is an offence punishable by a fine and/or imprisonment.

CONTRACT
A legally binding agreement between two or more people, each of whom agrees to provide something in return for something else. A contract may be oral or written. When a term of a contract has been broken, this is called a breach of contract.

CONTRIBUTORY NEGLIGENCE
Negligence occurs when someone carelessly injures you or your property. If the injury has been partially caused by your own carelessness, this is contributory negligence. If the judge finds that you have been contributorily negligent, the amount of your damages' award will be reduced by the amount for which you were to blame.

CORPORATION
A business formed according to certain legal requirements. Corporations are "persons" in law and can sue, be sued, sign contracts, etc., in the same manner as individuals.

Once a business has been incorporated, the individuals who run the business are protected from any personal liability. Only the business assets are available to "satisfy" any "judgments" obtained against the corporation. Besides business corporations, there are "Crown" corporations and charitable (non-profit) corporations. A crown corporation is a company through which the federal or provincial government carries on activities.

COSTS
A sum of money awarded by a court order to a "party" toward payment of the party's legal expenses.

COUNSEL
Lawyers.

COUNTERCLAIM
A claim against the plaintiff by the defendant. Generally, it will contain statements designed to counteract the claim made by the plaintiff against the defendant. It is not a "defence," but it is often included as part of the defence.

COURTHOUSE
A building with courtrooms in it.

CREDITOR
Generally, any person to whom money is owed. In small claims matters, any person who has obtained a judgment which has not yet been "satisfied."

CRIMINAL LAW
The body of law under which the "Crown" prosecutes persons who violate criminal laws.

CROSS-CLAIM
A claim by one defendant against another (see Counterclaim).

CROWN
The federal and provincial governments.

DAMAGES
Loss, injury, or deterioration to a person or a person's property, the extent or amount of which must be determined by the court. It must be distinguished from a debt which is a specific, known amount of money. If a person borrows money from a bank, he or she knows that if that money is not paid back, that specific amount of money plus interest will be owed. That is debt. If a person makes a contract to repair the watch of another person and does it in a careless manner, he or she may know that some money is owed to that person, but does not know the exact amount, and only the court can determine that amount. That is damages.

DEBT
A sum of money due by a certain and expressed agreement, where the amount is fixed and specific and does not depend on any subsequent evaluations by the court to settle it.

DEBTOR
Generally, any person who owes money. In small claims matters, a person who has not yet "satisfied" a judgment obtained against him or her.

DEBTOR EXAMINATION
(see Examination of Debtor)

DEFAULT JUDGMENT
Judgment given to the plaintiff when the defendant fails to defend the plaintiff's claim. No trial takes place. Available in cases of "debt" or "liquidated damages."

DEFENCE
The formal denial of the plaintiff's claim, which is filed by the defendant in the appropriate court office and sent to the plaintiff (formerly called a "dispute").

DEFENDANT
A person who is being sued.

DELIVERY
"Pleadings" have been delivered when they have been served and filed in the court office.

DEPONENT
The person who swears (makes) an affidavit.

DIRECT EXAMINATION
"Examination" by a party of his or her own witnesses (also called "examination-in-chief").

DIRECTOR
Directors of corporations are people elected by the shareholders of a corporation to manage its business affairs.

DISABILITY
(see Party under Disability)

DISBURSEMENTS
Legal expenses other than counsel fees, such as photocopying costs and court fees for service, filing, etc.

DISCONTINUANCE
Where the plaintiff voluntarily puts an end to his or her action, or the defendant abandons his or her defence.

DISCOVERY
A procedure by which a party can obtain information about an opposing party's case prior to trial. It may take place through written questions and answers or by oral questioning before a "special examiner." Very rarely ordered in small claims actions. Also known as an "examination for discovery."

DISCRETION
Judicial discretion is the power of a judge to decide on a course of action in regard to a legal problem. Discretion must be exercised within the limits of the law.

DISMISSAL
Denial of a claim.

DISPUTE
(see Defence)

DIVISIONAL COURT
A branch of the Supreme Court of Ontario, which hears, among other things, appeals from judgments of the small claims court.

ENCUMBRANCE
A liability attached to legal ownership of property. For example, a "mortgage."

ENTERED
Recorded in the court's files. The clerk enters "judgments" and other "orders."

EVIDENCE
Information, other than "argument," which tends to prove or disprove an "allegation" of a fact that is disputed in a case. Evidence is "admitted" by the court.

EXAMINATION
Generally, questioning.

EXAMINATION FOR DISCOVERY
(see Discovery)

EXAMINATION-IN-CHIEF
(see Direct Examination)

EXAMINATION OF DEBTOR
A procedure by which a creditor questions a debtor as to his or her financial circumstances (formerly called a judgment summons or "J.S."). The debtor is summoned to the hearing with a notice of examination (formerly called a "show cause summons").

EXECUTION
The formal signing of a legal document. It was also formerly used to mean action taken by the bailiff under a "writ of seizure and sale."

EXHIBIT
A document or other thing that has been admitted as evidence by a judge during a trial becomes marked as an exhibit. Documents that are attached to affidavits are also called exhibits.

EX PARTE PROCEEDINGS
"Proceedings" initiated by a party without notifying (e.g., by notice of motion) the opposing party.

EXPERT EVIDENCE
"Evidence" that is given by a person who is qualified in some special area of knowledge, such as medicine, cooking or car repair.

FACTS
Whatever "evidence" is believed by the judge or agreed to as true by the parties becomes the basis for the facts that are found to be true in the case. The judgment arises out of these facts.

FILING
A document is filed when it is delivered to a court office and accepted by the clerk.

FORUM
Place. The forum of a small claims court action is the small claims court in which it is to be heard.

GARNISHEE
A person who owes money to a debtor and is instructed by the court to pay the money to the court rather than to the debtor. The procedure by which this occurs is called garnishment.

GROUNDS
The reasons and legal basis for a request that is made by "motion."

HEARING
The presentation of evidence and/or argument to a judge at a "trial" or on a "motion."

INDEMNIFICATION
Repayment, reimbursement.

INTERIM
In the meantime. An interim order is one which is made prior to the trial.

ISSUE
A fact or matter of law which is in dispute is called a factual or legal issue.

ISSUED
A claim which has been served and filed is given a court case number. At this point, the claim has been issued.

J.S.
(see Examination of Debtor)

JUDGMENT
The final decision of the judge handed down after a trial. The judgment contains an award of "damages" and "costs."

JUDGMENT CREDITOR
(see Creditor)

JUDGMENT DEBTOR
(see Debtor)

JUDGMENT SUMMONS
(see Examination of Debtor)

JURISDICTION
Power. The small claims court's jurisdiction is limited as to what types of actions it may hear and what amount of money it may award.

LAND REGISTRY OFFICE
Keeps records of most of the land in southern Ontario.

LAND TITLES OFFICE
Keeps records of most of the land in northern Ontario.

LAW SOCIETY OF UPPER CANADA
The governing body of the legal profession in Ontario. It is composed of all practising lawyers and run by representatives, called benchers, who are elected by the members. The name gives you an idea of how long this institution has been around.

LEAVE
Permission of a judge.

LIABILITY
Legal responsibility.

LIMITATION PERIOD
A period of time set by legislation after which a right of action will be lost. Its purpose is to protect people against having the threat of a lawsuit hanging over their heads forever.

LIQUIDATED DAMAGES AND CLAIMS
Where a claim is for a specific amount of money that can be easily ascertained using objective data, such as a loan document, it is liquidated. If a claim is not liquidated, the amount of damages must be determined by a judge. A liquidated claim is a "debt." (See also "damages.")

LITIGANT
A "party."

LITIGATION
Litigation is the carrying out of a lawsuit.

LITIGATION GUARDIAN
A person appointed by the court to look after the legal interests of a "party under disability."

MONETARY JURISDICTION
(see Jurisdiction)

MORTGAGE
In the Land Registry system, a legal pledge of the title to land as security ("collateral") for money borrowed by a mortgagor from a mortgagee.

MOTION
A hearing before a judge to decide whether a party is entitled to a right he or she is asserting, other than the right to judgment itself.

NOTICE
A document which is "served" on one or more of the parties informing them of a step that has been taken in their action.

ORDER
A decision of the court resulting from a motion or trial. Decisions may be "interim" or final. A "judgment" is a final order. In the small claims court, only final orders may be appealed.

PARTICULARS
Details. For example, if you received a claim or a defence which was extremely vague, you might bring a motion for particulars.

PARTNERSHIP
A business partnership is a joint enterprise of two or more persons for the purpose of making a profit.

PARTY
Not necessarily as much fun as it sounds. A person named in a lawsuit. Plaintiffs, defendants and third parties are parties.

PARTY UNDER DISABILITY
A "party" who lacks legal capacity to sue or be sued without the assistance of a "litigation guardian."

PEREMPTORY ADJOURNMENT
(see Adjournment)

PERSON
A legal person is an entity which may take on legal rights and responsibilities and sue and be sued in its own name. Individuals and corporations are persons.

PERSONAL PROPERTY
All goods which are owned. Does not include land and items which are viewed as part of the land, such as buildings. These are known as real property.

PERSONAL SERVICE
(see Service)

PLAINTIFF
The person who launches a lawsuit by suing a "defendant."

PLEADINGS
The written statements, such as claims and defences, which are exchanged by parties during a lawsuit.

POST-JUDGMENT INTEREST
Interest on a judgment from the date the judgment is given until the date when the "debtor" "satisfies" the judgment.

PRAYER FOR RELIEF
The clause in a claim in which the plaintiff states what relief he or she is asking for. Usually this relief is in the form of damages, interest and costs.

PRE-JUDGMENT INTEREST
On a "liquidated claim," interest is due on the amount awarded from the date the debt became due up to the date of the judgment. On an unliquidated claim, interest is given from the date the plaintiff gave the defendant written notice of his or her claim up until the date of the judgment.

PREJUDICE
Injury. If a "party" has been prejudiced, this means the party has been hampered in handling its case.

PRE-TRIAL CONFERENCE
A meeting held prior to trial between the "parties" and a court official at which the parties exchange information and discuss the possibility of settling their case.

PROCEEDING
Actions and motions are proceedings.

PROPRIETORSHIP
(see Sole Proprietorship)

QUASH
Disallow. For example, appeals may be quashed.

REFEREE
A court official who conducts "pre-trial conferences," "damage" assessment hearings and other such proceedings.

REGISTRY OFFICE
(see Land Registry Office)

REGULATION
A legal rule made by cabinet as empowered by a "statute." Many of the rules of the small claims court are contained in regulations.

RES JUDICATA
A matter already decided.

RESERVED DECISION
The postponing of the making of an order by a judge.

RETRIAL
A new trial of a case which has already been tried and in which a judgment has been handed down.

RETURN DATE
(see Return of the Motion)

RETURN OF THE MOTION
The date on which a motion is to be heard.

RIGHT OF ACTION
(see Cause of Action)

SATISFACTION
When the "debtor" pays the "creditor" the full amount owing on a judgment, then the judgment (and hopefully the creditor as well) has been satisfied.

SEIZURE
The taking of a property by a bailiff or sheriff under a writ.

SERVICE
Delivery of a claim or other court document to a party or witness. Personal service is by hand delivery. Service may also occur by mail or advertisement or in some other manner designed to bring the document to the attention of a certain person.

SET-OFF
The balancing off of a debt owed by the plaintiff to the defendant with a debt owed by the defendant to the plaintiff.

SHERIFF
Sheriffs are similar to "bailiffs," but have greater "jurisdiction." For example, sheriffs may seize and sell land under a writ while bailiffs cannot.

SHOW CAUSE SUMMONS
(see Examination of Debtor)

SOLE PROPRIETORSHIP
An unincorporated business owned by an individual and registered either under his or her name or a business name.

SPECIAL EXAMINER
A person who is in the business of conducting "examinations."

STATEMENT OF CLAIM
(see Claim)

STATEMENT OF DEFENCE
(see Defence)

STATUTE
A provincial statute is a set of laws passed by a provincial legislature. Also called an act.

STAY
Proceedings are stayed when they are halted by a court order.

SUBPOENA
(see Summons)

SUMMONS
A legal document which commands the person to whom it is directed to appear in court to answer questions (also known as a subpoena).

TAXATION OF COSTS
(see Assessment)

TERRITORIAL DIVISION
A geographic area of the province. Offices of the small claims court are located in each division.

TESTIMONY
Evidence given orally by a witness under oath in a court.

THIRD PARTY
A person who was not sued by the plaintiff who is joined to the action by the defendant.

TITLE
Legal ownership.

TORT
A civil wrong which gives rise to a "cause of action." Torts include assault, battery, trespass, negligence, false imprisoment and the intentional infliction of mental suffering.

TRANSCRIPT
A typewritten record of testimony, argument, examinations and other legal proceedings.

TRIAL
An examination of and decision on a matter of law by a court.

TRUE COPY
A copy of a document without original signatures and seals.

UNLIQUIDATED DAMAGES
The opposite of "liquidated damages." (See also Damages.)

WARRANT OF COMMITTAL
Written authority given by a judge to arrest a person.

WITHOUT PREJUDICE
When this is written on a document, the author intends that the document is not to be used as evidence in court. Often settlement negotiations are conducted "without prejudice" to the plaintiff's right to proceed to court.

WRIT OF DELIVERY
A document issued by the court commanding a person to give up possession of certain property.

WRIT OF SEIZURE AND SALE
A document issued by the court authorizing the bailiff to take possession of and sell property owned by a "debtor" in "satisfaction" of a judgment.

TITLES AVAILABLE
FROM
SELF-COUNSEL PRESS

LEGAL TITLES

CIVIL RIGHTS
An excellent guide to Canadian civil rights, this book covers many offences punishable under summary conviction as well as the more serious criminal offences. It has been updated to explain the effect of the new Charter of Rights and Freedoms.

THE CONSUMER BOOK
Consumer's rights under the various consumer protection acts and federal legislation are carefully explained and practical tips are provided on how "victims" can protect themselves.

CREDIT, DEBT, AND BANKRUPTCY
This handbook is for persons who buy on credit, which includes just about all of us. It suggests how to handle debt harassment, debt pooling, and bankruptcy.

CRIMINAL PROCEDURE IN CANADA
For the lawyer, police officer, or anyone who has more than the occasional involvement with the courts, this book is an invaluable ready reference guide.

DIVORCE GUIDE
Our *Divorce Guide* is the original do-it-yourself aid. It is the most complete and up-to-date publication available on how to obtain an uncontested divorce.

FOR SALE BY OWNER
If you want to save thousands of dollars on real estate commissions when you sell your home, this book will tell you the proven techniques you need to know in order to succeed.

IMMIGRATING TO CANADA
This guide explains how the Canadian immigration system works and how to become a legal immigrant. Examples of application forms are included.

IMMIGRATING TO THE U.S.A.
Written by a lawyer specializing in immigration, this is a complete guide to how to immigrate to the U.S. It is useful for the prospective immigrant and for relatives in the U.S. who are trying to help.

LANDLORDING IN CANADA
Whether you plan to rent out an apartment, house, or condominium, this comprehensive guide explains both the practical and legal aspects you need to know.

LANDLORD/TENANT RIGHTS
This book provides both the landlord and the tenant with a working knowledge of the law in the landlord/tenant relationship. Areas covered include tenancy agreements, rent increases, security deposits, repairs, right to privacy, and evictions.
Not available for all provinces. See order form.

MARRIAGE & FAMILY LAW
Of particular interest to women, this book deals with all aspects of the marriage and family institution and explains how to use the law to protect your rights.
Not available for all provinces. See order form.

MEDIA LAW HANDBOOK
Every person in the news industry and every book author or publisher will find this book invaluable. The structure of the Canadian news industry is given as a background to a concise discussion of CRTC regulations, copyright laws, reporting on criminal trials, and much more.

MEDICAL LAW HANDBOOK
This book introduces you to the rules that bind health-care workers and tells you what to do if you are caught in a legal battle.

MORTGAGES AND FORECLOSURE
This book cuts through the legal jargon of a home mortgage contract and explains what should and shouldn't concern the buyer. It describes different types of mortgages available in today's market and how to use a mortgage as an investment.

PHOTOGRAPHY AND THE LAW
Whether you are a professional or a hobbyist, here are the rules on what can be photographed, how a photograph can be taken, and how and when it can be used.

PROBATE GUIDE
This book shows, in non-technical language, how to apply for and obtain letters probate or administration and transfer the assets to the beneficiaries, without the help or cost of a lawyer.
Not available in all provinces. See order form.

REAL ESTATE BUYING/SELLING GUIDE
The author includes an excellent introduction to the general area of real estate as well as a discussion of commercial mortgages, government loans and grants, and sale and purchase of real estate.
Not available in all provinces. See order form.

USING THE ACCESS TO INFORMATION ACT
The clear, simplified instructions for using the new law will be most valuable to journalists, researchers, political scientists, teachers, and consumer advocates who need to cut through government red tape to gain access to the vast amounts of available information.

WILLS
This book explains the whys and hows of writing a will and indicates the complications that arise in relation to wills and estate planning.
Not available for all provinces. See order form.

PERSONAL HELP TITLES

AIDS TO INDEPENDENCE
This book is a comprehensive catalogue of products available to help the disabled and elderly function effectively and live a full and satisfying life. Black and white photographs illustrate the aids.

BETWEEN THE SEXES
Whether you've been together two years or twenty, this book is designed to help you break through the cycles of frustration or anger in your relationship and work toward a positive lifestyle.

FAMILY TIES THAT BIND
This book explains a proven approach for dealing with the complications of family relationships and establishing more positive directions in your life.

MANAGING STRESS
This book covers general health and well-being, personal planning skills, communication skills, quieting, autogenic methods, and progressive relaxation training. Each technique helps take the worry out of worrying.

A PARENTS' GUIDE TO DAY CARE
This comprehensive consumer's guide to child care alternatives shows parents how to inform themselves about the choices and how to make day care a positive experience.

RETIREMENT GUIDE
For those who are unprepared, retirement is both a shock and a disappointment. This guide gives counsel on how to prepare for a healthy, happy, and financially secure retirement.

TAKING CARE
Practical advice for anyone in a prolonged situation of caretaking an adult relative or spouse.

WORKING COUPLES
Being a working couple doesn't have to mean having constant conflict in your life. This practical guide takes a straightforward approach to the issues involved when both people in a relationship are working outside the home.

CAREER DEVELOPMENT AND REFERENCE

THE HANDY GUIDE TO ABBREVIATIONS AND ACRONYMS FOR THE AUTOMATED OFFICE
Over 7000 abbreviations and acronyms commonly used in the fields of computers, law, business, and medicine are defined.

ASKING QUESTIONS
Entertaining, informative guide to the art of the interview based on the experience of dozens of well-known interviewers.

BETTER BOOK FOR GETTING HIRED
The focus of this book is on the importance of the resume. You may be short changing yourself by not giving the prospective employer an accurate picture of your talents.